TWELVE
TRAPS
IN TODAY'S
MARRIAGE

TWELVE
TRAPS
IN TODAY'S
MARRIAGE

and how to avoid them

Brent A. Barlow

Deseret Book Company
Salt Lake City, Utah

MACES III (Marital Adaptability and Cohesion Evaluation Scale), developed by David H. Olson, Joyce Portner, and Yoav Lavee, Family Social Science, 290 McNeal Hall, University of Minnesota, St. Paul, MN 55108. Copyright ©1985 D. H. Olson. Used by permission.

"On Nest Building." From Carol Lynn Pearson, *The Flight and the Nest*, Bookcraft, 1975. Copyright by Bookcraft, Inc., 1975. Used with permission.

"Patti Perfect" reprinted from *Exponent II* with permission of the copyright holders Margaret B. Black and Midge W. Nielsen.

Excerpts from *ACME Marriage Enrichment* newsletter used by permission of *ACME Marriage Enrichment*, 459 South Church St., P.O. Box 10596, Winston-Salem, NC 27108.

Excerpts from *Couples: How to Confront Problems and Maintain Loving Relationships*. COPYRIGHT ©1979 by Dr. Carlfred B. Broderick. Reprinted by permission of SIMON & SCHUSTER, Inc.

Excerpts from *Marriage Encounter* magazine used by permission of *Marriage Encounter*, 955 Lake Drive, St. Paul, MN 55120.

Excerpts reprinted with permission of Macmillan Publishing Company from *How to Speak, How to Listen*. Copyright ©1983 by Mortimer J. Adler.

Excerpts taken from *Love and Anger in Marriage*, by David R. Mace. Copyright ©1982 by The Zondervan Corporation. Used by permission.

Excerpts taken from *The Act of Marriage*, by Tim & Beverly LaHaye. Copyright ©1976 by The Zondervan Corporation. Used by permission.

Excerpts adapted from *Be Good to Each Other: An Open Letter on Marriage* by Lowell and Carol Erdahl. Copyright ©1976 by Lowell and Carol Erdahl. A Hawthorn book. Reprinted by permission of E. P. Dutton, a division of New American Library.

First printing August 1986
Second printing January 1987

Library of Congress Cataloging-in-Publication Data

Barlow, Brent A., 1941–
 Twelve traps in today's marriage and how to
avoid them.

 Bibliography: p.
 Includes index.
 1. Marriage—Religious aspects—Church of Jesus Christ
of Latter-day Saints. 2. Church of Jesus Christ of
Latter-day Saints—Doctrines. 3. Mormon Church—
Doctrines. I. Title. II. Title: 12 traps in
today's marriage and how to avoid them.
BX8641.B29   1986   248.4'8933204   86-13429
ISBN 0-87579-039-9

CONTENTS

v

CONTENTS

vi

PREFACE

Suppose for a moment you are the production manager in a large factory that makes farm tractors. For years you have produced tractors with a guarantee that each will last the owner's lifetime. Your tractors are superior products, highly sought after and very capable. Seldom do you have a tractor returned because it fails to meet the expectations and demands of those who utilize it.

Then, for reasons not entirely known, the owners begin to return their tractors more frequently for repairs. Large numbers of tractors begin to break down. As production manager, you become concerned and start an investigation. For years you have produced the same tractors with the same design, the same motors, and the same capabilities. Nothing as yet has had to be changed on the assembly line.

Even the most satisfied of your former customers start returning their tractors. New customers even bring back their tractors after just a few months. Tractors of the old design start breaking down in record numbers before the lifetime warranty has expired. Ultimately forty percent of the tractors you produce are returned, and reports arrive that many of the tractors remaining in the field are barely surviving. Numerous other owners are quite dissatisfied.

As production manager, what would you do? Would you continue to produce tractors of the same vintage and design with a failure rate of forty percent? Or would you redesign the tractor? Would you go into the field and watch the tractors at work? Would you carefully examine the ones that are returned to see why they have ceased to function?

After locating certain problems, would you issue an alert to other tractor owners to avoid similar difficulties? Would you examine the work demands of the tractors and calculate stress points and limitations? Would you possibly consider revising and updating your tractors? Would you determine how much demands have increased over the years and whether the owners have properly cared for their tractors and provided even routine maintenance?

Or would you ignore the forty percent failure rate and go right on producing the same old tractor?

Why We Need Information about Contemporary Marriage

Some people, particularly husbands, are reluctant to admit that we need education about marriage today. After all, our parents and particularly our grandparents did not have it and supposedly did not need it. This kind of logic has a definition. According to Dr. Clark Vincent, marriage educator and counselor, it is called the "myth of naturalism." Simply defined, the myth of naturalism implies that human beings take to marriage as naturally as little ducks take to water. It is all somehow instinctive, effortless, and automatic.

The idea that our parents and grandparents didn't have to learn about marriage, and that therefore neither do we, is also an illusion. Our ancestors had different expectations about marriage. It was just something a person did that stayed done. Furthermore, people of a few decades ago may have been willing to put up with some circumstances in marriage that few would tolerate today.

In addition, I believe marriage is much more complex today than it has been in times past. We now confront issues and situations that our progenitors may not have experienced. With these thoughts in mind, I have written *Twelve Traps in Today's Marriage*. I firmly believe that many married couples today unknowingly get into situations—traps, if you will—that can be harmful to marriage. This may be out of ignorance, apathy, or innocence, or any combination of the three.

Through marriage counseling sessions and through discussions during the many marriage seminars I have con-
ducted, I have become aware of many of these traps. Susan
and I have even encountered some of them in our own marital
relationship. In *Twelve Traps in Today's Marriage* I have identified what I believe to be twelve major traps in contemporary
marriage. Obviously, there are others, and all do not start
with the letter *T*, but I have attempted to identify the major
ones and alert others to the dangers. And to those who may
be presently snared, I hope the book will help them find a
way out.

Trap: Any device, stratagem, trick, or the like for catching
a person unawares.

ACKNOWLEDGMENTS

I would like to acknowledge and sincerely thank the following people on the staff of Deseret Book for helping to make this book a reality: Richard Tice, editor; Kent Ware, design director; Karen Morales, design assistant, Linda Egbert, typesetter; Charlotte Carpenter, proofreader; Richard Bingham, marketing manager; Eleanor Knowles, publishing manager; and Ronald Millett, president of Deseret Book. I would also like to recognize and extend my thanks to the Faculty Support Center at Brigham Young University for assistance in preparing the manuscript.

I would especially like to thank my children for their patience once again during another writing project. And to my wife, Susan, I express my deepest love and appreciation not only for her encouragement, help, and assistance in writing this book, but also for her willingness to share so much of our marriage in the pages that follow.

"Thus he flattereth them, and leadeth them along until he draggeth their souls down to hell; and thus he causeth them to catch themselves in their own snare."

D&C 10:26

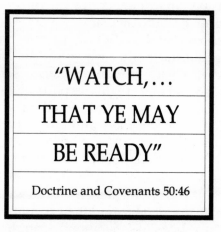

> # "WATCH,...
> # THAT YE MAY
> # BE READY"
>
> Doctrine and Covenants 50:46

Watch: To be attentive or vigilant; to keep guard; to keep someone or something under close observation.

WATCHING AND BEING READY: *Becoming knowledgeable about our marriage and not letting either ignorance or Satan undermine it.*

A few months ago a student asked if he could talk to me during my office hours. He was a handsome, intelligent young man who was planning to marry in a few months. In my office he told me that, after nearly thirty years of marriage, his parents were getting a divorce. He said that "it is one thing to get a divorce after several years of struggling with a bad relationship. But my parents had a picture-perfect marriage all the years I was growing up. We had a large LDS family, a hard-working father, a sensitive, concerned mother, and all of us regularly participated in Church activities." In fact, all the sons had served missions, and the young man's four older brothers and sisters had married in the temple.

"How could a divorce happen?" he asked.

I've had that kind of conversation more than once during the past few years. Too often young men and women who are in the transition to married life find their parents in the transition out of it. These late-life separations occur despite the fact that the parents appear to have fine marital relationships. And the question—"How could a divorce occur?"—is asked time and time again.

I told the young man that I didn't know the reasons why picture-perfect marriages sometimes come unframed and end in divorce. But I have since started to form some opinions centered around the picture-perfect marriage concept. Many believe, or are misled to believe, that they do have ideal marital relationships. Furthermore, if they believe they have such fine marriage relationships, they may think they don't have to do anything to keep them. That may just be the difference between a marriage that lasts and one that does not.

Another LDS man once sent me a letter that described a similar situation. He had been married several years and thought that he too had the picture-perfect marriage. During twelve years of marriage and five children, his wife had not said one thing to indicate that their marriage was anything less than near perfect. They had had no arguments, no complaints, no differences of opinion that had even insinuated

2

anything was wrong; and because of this, he thought the marriage was going well. Then, on the twelfth wedding anniversary, she walked into the room and handed him an envelope. Thinking it was an anniversary card, he opened it. Much to his surprise, it was legal papers for divorce proceedings.

The man mentioned in his letter that the reason he and his wife, and perhaps many others, divorced is because they did not think divorce could happen to them. Consequently, they had let their guards down (or didn't keep them up), and the blows followed.

Someone once observed that it is better for a person to have a heart attack and then learn to take care of his health than to live on in the ignorance that he has heart problems. So it is with marriage. Working to improve a somewhat less-than-perfect marriage may be far more sound than living under the illusion that we have the ideal marital relationship. Under such an illusion, we believe we don't have to do anything for our marriage as the years pass by. Picture-perfect marriages, whatever they are, can fail, and in this book we are going to find out why and what might be done to prevent failure.

A Myth about Marriage

Susan and I spent the first three months of our marriage living in Centerfield, Utah (population then was 600). I ran my Dad's service station during that time. The first three weeks of our marriage were total bliss—just like in the movies. That was how we thought marriage should be. Then, toward the end of the first month of marriage we had a disagreement, nothing of major significance. Right now I can't even remember what it was about.

After the conflict was settled, we were thoroughly dejected. Happily married couples, so we thought, didn't have disagreements. We had both entered marriage with that belief. So after we had our "encounter of the first kind," we thought there was little hope for our marriage.

3

What hopes we did have were then dashed the following Sunday when an elderly gentleman stood up in church and informed us that he and his wife had lived fifty years without so much as a cross word. Susan and I had made it for only three weeks. While walking home from church we wondered out loud if any of our friends ever had any kind of confrontations or disagreements. But we didn't dare ask.

At that point we believed a seriously misleading marriage myth. We thought that if we married the right person we would live happily ever after. Like ourselves, many married couples might be led to believe that happily married couples don't experience any conflicts or disappointments in life. We thought that a successful marriage was one in which the couple did not have any problems. Later on in our marriage, we realized that a successful marriage is actually one in which the couple learn to deal with and solve the problems they inevitably have. The real test in marriage, therefore, is confronting rather than running from the daily demands and difficulties in life.

Susan and I later learned to appreciate the statement of C. G. Jung, who observed, "All those for whom marriage contains no problems are not living in the present."

No Couple Immune

When I was working on my doctoral degree in marriage counseling at Florida State University, I took a course titled "The Family in the United States." It was an excellent course taught by one of the most competent professors in family studies in the country.

During the course he once made the statement that "no couple in the United States today [that was 1970] is immune from divorce or marital failure." I was quite startled and taken aback by the statement. Certainly I felt secure in my own marriage and knew numerous LDS married couples whom I would deem "immune from divorce." After class I took the opportunity to challenge my professor on his statement, but he stood his ground. I tried to explain to him about temple

4

marriage and its security. He already knew I was a Latter-day Saint and said his observation was true for Mormon couples as well. He rephrased his original statement to say, "No married couple, including Latter-day Saints, is immune from divorce or marital failure."

I never forgot his statement, nor did I repeat it for another ten years. I simply did not believe it. I felt there was some security in temple marriage that would put marital turmoil beyond LDS people. But during the following decade I began to be more observant and noted some interesting things happening.

In one LDS ward where we were living, there were four couples who divorced within an eighteen-month period. All the husbands had served missions, all the couples had married in the temple, all had children, and all were currently participating in Church activities. Other couples we knew also divorced, while some indicated that they were quite dissatisfied with their marriages.

I am impressed and even encouraged when I realize how well the vast majority of LDS couples are coping and getting along despite the marital disruption that surrounds us. Nevertheless, I am now convinced that my professor at Florida State University was correct: At the present time no married couple in the United States, including Latter-day Saint couples, is immune from marital turmoil.

I saw my professor at the National Council on Family Relations in Milwaukee, Wisconsin, during October 1983 and asked him if he still believed that no couple is immune. He said yes, even more so today.

On November 5, 1983, I was speaking to an LDS group in Salt Lake City on marriage. At that time I mentioned that I did not know what the divorce rate was among Latter-day Saints because the Church had not disclosed those statistics. But I stated then that the divorce rate in the United States was about 40 percent, and I estimated it could be as high as 25 percent in our church. That was on a Friday night.

The next day, on November 6, we received our copy of the

Church News, which contained an article with some interesting statistics on divorce among Latter-day Saints. The article stated, according to one study, that about one-third of the Church members between the ages of eighteen and thirty will have experienced divorce by the time they reach sixty. The rate for those married in the temple, however, is much less. It was also estimated that 49 percent of all LDS women will be single before age 65. About 35 percent will divorce, 11 percent will be widowed, and approximately 3 percent will not marry. (Van Leer, p. 4. See the *Ensign,* July 1984, pp. 78-80, for additional statistics on Church marriage and divorce.)

The Danger of the Ditch

A few years ago my wife and I moved to a new community into a subdivision that was not yet completed. There was a large ditch full of water that ran directly in front of the home we wanted to buy. We contacted the city engineers, and they promised to put in a culvert and cover the ditch, though the project would take approximately three months to complete.

So Susan and I faced a real problem. The delay meant we would have to live with our five small children in constant fear and real danger of the ditch full of water. We had the option of renting another home until the ditch was covered; or we could purchase the home, move in, and live with the danger until it passed.

We deliberated over the options for some time. In hindsight perhaps it was a great risk, but we bought the home and moved in. By so doing we decided we would have to keep ourselves and our children constantly aware of the danger of the ditch. We had frequent discussions on how we would keep our children away from the dangerous water. We took them out by the bank of the ditch and explained how they could be harmed if they were not careful. Susan and I took turns being around the yard during that summer when our children and others were playing near, and sometimes in, the water. We asked the older children to help watch out for the younger ones. The danger of the ditch was real.

We often prayed as a family that Heavenly Father would watch over us during our daily activities and that "no harm or accident would come to any of us," words that became very significant in our lives. Susan and I prayed together too for the safety of our children. And one night at midnight I went out by the ditch and alone prayed on the bank of the ditch for the safety of everyone who might possibly be harmed by the dangerous conditions.

The days, weeks, and then the summer finally passed by. The city engineers were good on their word, and within three months the culvert was in, the ditch covered, and the danger was past.

During that summer, however, we learned an interesting and significant lesson: *Those most aware of the danger are often the ones least harmed!*

Since we lived right next to the bank of the ditch, we were the ones in the neighborhood most aware and fearful of it. Those who lived greater distances away seemed to be less aware of the danger and less concerned about the potential problems. Since we lived next to the ditch, we moved up to the bank and stood guard. And no one was harmed.

In August 1984 I was speaking on marriage relationships to an LDS group in Belfast, Ireland, and related the Danger of the Ditch story. I shared with them my insight that those closest to the danger are often the safest because they stand guard. After my speech a mother came up and said she also believed in that principle. Her son was a member of the Royal Ulster police and was in constant confrontation with the Irish Republican Army from the south of Ireland. She said she always felt better when he was on duty patrolling the border because he wore his flak jacket and was on guard for both himself and his buddies. She feared most for his life when he returned to police barracks in Belfast and let down his guard. She too believed that those most aware of the danger are often the ones least harmed.

I think this may be a lesson for contemporary marriages. Those most aware of factors contributing to marital failure

7

may be the ones least affected. We must move up to the edge of the danger, put on our flak jackets, and stand guard. In the recent past I have had the opportunity to speak to two LDS groups who literally live in marital danger zones: Las Vegas, Nevada, and Orange County, California. As most readers are aware, Las Vegas is the divorce capital of the United States. Though many out-of-state couples go to Las Vegas for divorces, Latter-day Saints in that area nonetheless live in or near a city that accounts for numerous divorces each year.

The other group in Orange County lives in an area where divorce is now the norm—where more couples divorce than stay married. But as I spoke to these two groups on different occasions, I had the distinct impression that the LDS couples in these communities were safer than the groups I had addressed who lived in other areas. The Latter-day Saints in Las Vegas and in Orange County were living near the ditch, but I observed that they had moved up to the bank and were standing guard.

Two Great Messages

There are two great messages of The Church of Jesus Christ of Latter-day Saints related to marriage. One is that the restored gospel can bind married couples together for eternity. Of all the doctrines we teach, this has to be one of the most comforting and most reassuring. The second is implied by the first: that the restored gospel of Jesus Christ can bind couples together for mortality as well. Without the latter there is no guarantee of the former.

If an LDS couple marries in the temple and then later chooses to divorce civilly, I honestly do not know if or under what circumstances they would be together in the next life. I will leave that question to our Church leaders and theologians. But another major concern I have is about those troubled couples who do not divorce but live their marriages in quiet desperation. Though their marriages have been sealed in the temple, some couples are not necessarily happy and are doing little or nothing about their circumstances.

8

Some mistakenly think, I believe, that even though they are not happy now, something magic will happen in the resurrection, and they will be happy there. Whether or not this is true, I do not know either.

The Book of Mormon teaches that the "same spirit which doth possess your bodies at the time that ye go out of this life, that same spirit will have power to possess your body in that eternal world." (Alma 34:34.) I hope I do not misinterpret this scripture, but it seems to me that how we end up in this life, in our personalities and in our relationships, is how we will at least begin in the next one. Moroni similarly teaches that in the hereafter "he that is happy shall be happy still; and he that is unhappy shall be unhappy still." (Morm. 9:14.) What kind of marital relationship we will have in the next life will be influenced, if not determined, in part by what kind of marriage we have here. That can either be good news or bad news, depending on one's situation.

But the definite good news is that we have time during mortality to work on our marriages. Bad marriages can become good, and good marriages can become better. LDS could also stand for LET'S DO SOMETHING! Let's do something about our marital relationships while we still have the opportunity and the time to do it. The Book of Mormon states that "this life is the time for men to prepare to meet God; yea, behold the day of this life is the day for men to perform their labors." (Alma 34:32.) Nothing could be closer to the truth than this statement in actively working on relationships that not only endure, but are also rewarding and fulfilling as well.

Weather Watch vs. Weather Warning

As a religious denomination we are doing quite well in marriage and in family matters, but we are not immune from the social turmoil of the times. The belief that we are, or will be, immune is one of the very reasons I believe we unnecessarily allow some things to happen in our midst. I appreciate now more than ever the statement of Nephi, "Wo be unto him that is at ease in Zion! Wo be unto him that crieth: All is well!"

9

(2 Ne. 28:24-25.) I am not one to cry "All is well in Zion." On the other hand, I am not willing to cry "All is not well" either. We as a church are doing remarkably well in many respects, but my suggestion is that we can and must do better if we do not want to be swept away in the current tides of social, and particularly marital, disruption.

During the past few years we have seen some unusual weather in the intermountain area. We have experienced an abundance of water; and floods and mud slides have consequently followed. Each evening during the flooding season I turned on the television set to get the weather report on what might happen that night, the following day, or the days to follow. I gained an appreciation of the weather service and their ability to anticipate and even predict certain weather conditions. During this time I learned the difference between a weather watch and a weather warning.

A *weather watch* means that inclement weather is on its way, and we should be aware of what is coming. A *weather warning* means the turbulent weather is upon us, and we should take precautionary measures to avoid the impact.

In a way, this book is a social weather watch to describe some conditions "out there" that are causing disruption for others. These conditions are heading our way and are even, to some degree, in our midst. In the pages that follow, I wish to point out some of the current trends in marital relationships and to indicate some ways I hope will help others to avoid these troubles.

If You Fear

You may have heard the following saying concerning our testimonies: "If you fear, then fear not. If you fear not, then fear." We should not become complacent about our testimonies of the gospel because we could, over time, lose them. If we are not fearful of losing our testimonies, we should be. They are indeed pearls of great price to be not only guarded but shared.

On the other hand, if we are fearful of losing our testimonies, we will likely not do so because we will take necessary precautions to prevent such a thing from happening. If we are fearful of losing them, we should "fear not." It probably won't happen because of our caution, concern, and activity.

Whenever I speak to LDS groups on marriage, I like to apply that quote on fear to marriage. I believe that LDS couples should be fearful of or concerned about detrimental influences and marital problems. We often think of marital disruption as something that happens to someone else. The reality is that *any* LDS marriage can be disrupted and end in divorce. And some do, I believe, partly because the couples "fear not." We must stand guard. These things are not supposed to happen to Latter-day Saints, but they can and sometimes do.

A Sign of the Times

One of the reasons I believe that so much marital disruption exists in the world today is because it may be a sign of the times. In Matthew 24:3 the disciples of Jesus asked about his second coming. They inquired of him, "Tell us, when shall these things be? and what shall be the sign of thy coming, and of the end of the world?"

Note his response in verse four: "Jesus answered and said unto them, Take heed that no man deceive you." Thus, according to Jesus, deception among the people of the world would be one of the signs Christ mentioned first. I believe many couples, including some among the Latter-day Saints, have been deceived into believing erroneous ideas about their marital relationships.

In other verses in Matthew 24, Jesus gave some additional signs of the times that I believe refer or relate to marriage. In verse ten he states, "Then shall many be offended, and shall betray one another, and shall hate one another." And in verse twelve he adds, "Because iniquity shall abound, the love of many shall wax cold."

But the verse that has the greatest significance for me is

11

Matthew 24:24, in which Jesus states that in the last days "if it were possible, they [meaning the deceivers] shall deceive the very elect." To whom was Jesus referring when he talked about the elect? The elect are likely to be found among all groups on the face of the earth, and surely many Latter-day Saints are among the elect. (See Matt. 24:31.) It is my own opinion that most couples married in the LDS temples are among the elect or have the potential to become such.

Jesus stated that in the last days the elect would be deceived—if it were possible. Notice that he did not say it would be automatic deception. He stated "if it were possible." I believe many LDS couples have been deceived or currently are being deceived about marital and family relationships. Because of this, many are divorcing, living in quiet desperation, or experiencing family trauma.

The Great Deceiver

Like many of you, I used to watch comedian Flip Wilson and his parody of "The devil made me do it." Obviously, the devil is not responsible for all divorces or everything else that goes wrong in life. But I honestly believe that we, as LDS couples, have not given adequate attention to what Satan, the great deceiver, is trying to do to our own marriages and families.

When Susan and I lived in Eau Claire, Wisconsin, I recall an elderly gentleman who drove ninety-five miles in a blizzard to speak to our ward one night in January. His entire speech was based on the theme "you don't have to be possessed by evil to be influenced by evil." His point was well stated.

Many of us may be reluctant or unwilling to admit that Satan is influencing us in our daily lives. However, if we are willing to take a careful look at our personal lives, our marriages, and our families, many of us can see where we may have been "influenced by evil." Satan is indeed actively at work in our midst, and once we become aware of his tactics, we can become even more knowledgeable of his involvement in contemporary affairs. Latter-day revelation indicates that Satan "maketh war with the saints of God, and encompasseth them round about." (D&C 76:29.)

It has always impressed me that whenever college football or basketball teams are about to compete with each other, they often obtain video tapes of the opposition, study them in detail, and outline some strategy for the upcoming competition. Perhaps we should also make a detailed study of how Satan operates so we may be better prepared.

Sometimes when I speak to different LDS groups about marriage, I mention Satan and his possible tactics. We then play a game called "If I Were the Devil." I ask them to pretend that they are called to be on the devil's committee to disrupt or terminate marriages in their particular vicinity. What would they do? After a few minutes of discussion they report back some very effective strategies. I then indicate what I would do to disrupt married couples if I were the devil. Here are some of the ideas I've collected:

If I Were the Devil

If I were the devil and wanted to mess up a lot of marriages, I would first start with the newlyweds and try to get them discouraged early in the relationship. As the marriage progressed, I would get both husband and wife involved in so many activities that they would be constantly exhausted, physically and mentally. Couples who are too tired to do much together really have no advantage over those who won't do things together, and fatigue and exhaustion are wonderful contributors to marital disruption. It would be much easier for me then to make those couples tense, snippy, and easy to anger.

If I were the devil and wanted to disrupt a lot of marriages, I would make many think that they are very secure in their marital relationships when in actuality they are not. That way they would probably not do much for their marriages. I would make them think that divorce is something that happens to everyone else. I would discourage any and all

13

attempts a couple might make to change any aspect of their marriage that they do not like. Growth, likewise, would be discouraged. I would try to prevent couples from obtaining counseling or any other outside help.

If I were the devil, I would invent a box about two feet square that married people, individually or collectively, would sit around and stare at for hours upon end and late into the night. This would help control any meaningful conversation that might otherwise occur. It would assure me that any potential time that might be spent together as husband and wife would otherwise be consumed by staring at my box.

I would make men and women believe that being a husband or wife is far less important than being a father or mother. Children must come first, even at the expense of the marriage. If I were the devil and wanted to mess up marriages, I would make married couples believe that if their sexual relationship is functioning well, all others will also. If that tactic did not work, I think I would go to the other extreme and get them to underestimate the importance of sexual interaction in marriage. Having a balance would then be very difficult to attain.

If I were the devil, I would also make in-laws believe that they must keep their married children very close to them in the name of family solidarity. I would have the in-laws insist that their married children visit often, whether they wanted to come or not. Then if the children, for whatever reason, did not come, I would encourage the in-laws to act offended in subtle ways. Guilt is a wonderful disrupter of contemporary marriages.

I would try to make people believe that more people are getting divorced than are staying married. I would try to make everyone believe that marriage is only for the young, that love is only for the beautiful and attractive, as defined by Madison Avenue. I would get them to feel dissatisfied with themselves and their spouses if they don't fit the image, and to think that midway through life, the best has passed them by. I'd hope that they would not only believe these things,

14

but would also act accordingly. And maybe they would think that behavior, like age, is unchangeable.

And finally, I would try to convince married couples that I really do not exist.

After sharing the foregoing thoughts with a group one time, I received this letter in the mail a few days later:

Dear Dr. Barlow:

I don't have to think about what I would do to ruin marriages if I were the devil, because I already know what he has done to try to ruin mine. Just three weeks ago I received a phone call from a stranger informing me that his wife and my husband were seeing each other. I, who was so sure this type of thing happened only to other people, trusted my husband completely and did not believe the stranger at first. But as evidence surfaced that same evening, I began to see that I might be wrong. And I was. My husband confirmed the stranger's story only hours after the man called.

Since that night a lot has happened, both good and bad. My eyes have been opened to the small things that happened over a period of a few years. All this led up to the situation of my husband having a relationship with another woman.

The devil is sly, cunning, and intelligent. Here are three things he did to try to ruin our marriage:

1. He made my husband believe that success in his job was more important than anything else. This resulted in many hours, sixty to seventy hours a week, spent away from home.

2. He made me believe that to compensate for my feelings of loneliness and rejection I was not to let my husband know that I cared about him. For revenge, I would not share my feelings with him or care what his feelings were; I would give all my love and time to our small children instead of to him (and then resent both the children and my husband). Also, I would not give him the physical love he needed, not only refraining from sexual relations but also from touching, kissing, sitting close, holding hands, and the like. And finally, I became so sure that all of our problems were his fault I stopped being willing to change or even to compromise in any manner.

15

3. He made my husband believe that there was no harm in having a close "friendly" relationship with a member of the opposite sex. (They were just helping each other with their problems in the beginning, but it ended up in a sexual relationship also.)

Through all of our troubles, with everything working against us, we have found strength in the LDS faith. We were both humbled and chastened, but are now able to apply the principles of the restored gospel in our relationship with each other. Eternity now looks a whole lot closer and brighter since we were able to regain the love we nearly lost.

I give the devil a lot of credit for our dilemma. But I am also thankful I can trust in the Lord for our present and future happiness.

Other Tactics of Satan

As previously noted in Doctrine and Covenants 76:29, Satan is at war with the Saints. Latter-day revelation also indicates that "the devil has sought to lay a cunning plan, that he may destroy [the Lord's] work." (D&C 10:12.) Among his major tactics is to convince people that he does not exist: "[Satan] saith unto them: I am no devil, for there is none— and thus he whispereth in their ears, until he grasps them with his awful chains, from whence there is no deliverance." (2 Ne. 28:22.) I know it may not sound professional for a university professor and licensed marriage counselor to blame much of our marital turmoil on the devil, but I am convinced that he has nearly succeeded in his effort to convince us of his supposed nonexistence. In fact, he has done it so effectively that many of us are no longer aware of his influence in our lives.

Another major tactic is to make men and women miserable. Satan is a miserable person, and "he seeketh that all men might be miserable like unto himself." (2 Ne. 2:27.) I'm not saying that every time we have a bad day it is the devil's fault. But I do know that when we are miserable, he does not mind, and we are in his camp. Remember, we do not have to

16

be possessed of evil to be influenced by evil. And if we are continually miserable, particularly in our marital and family relationships, I know that Satan is pleased about our condition and would prefer us to stay that way.

Still another tactic of Satan is that of stirring up contention, because "the devil . . . is the father of contention, and he stirreth up the hearts of men to contend with anger, one with another." (3 Ne. 11:29.) I am not implying that every little bit of discord in LDS marriages is caused by the devil. Normal family life usually contains some amount of discord— there is and will be sibling rivalry and competition among family members. My main concern is the contention that goes beyond what is normal. My wife and I have discussed this often with our children and have also talked about it in our marriage. Whenever we experience contention, we are moving away from the Lord in the direction of Satan and his plan. Married LDS couples who live in a constant state of contention ought to be aware of this particular tactic of Satan.

The Book of Mormon also gives three other tactics of Satan: anger, pacification, and flattery. Nephi, in speaking of the last days, states, "At that day shall he rage in the hearts of the children of men, and stir them up to anger against that which is good." (2 Ne. 28:20.) The topic of anger is significant enough, I believe, that I have devoted an entire chapter to it. (See "Trap 8: The Temper Trap.") But for now, suffice it to say that Satan would like to see Latter-day Saint couples become angry, particularly at their spouses. When we become angry, we say and do things we ordinarily would not—it is almost as if we become emotionally intoxicated.

Still another tactic of Satan is that of pacification or apathy. Nephi states, "Others will he pacify, and lull them away into carnal security, that they will say: All is well in Zion; yea, Zion prospereth, all is well—and thus the devil cheateth their souls, and leadeth them away carefully down to hell." (2 Ne. 28:21.) If he can't get us one way, he'll try another.

Of the two tactics, anger and apathy (or pacification), I

17

believe Satan uses the last one most effectively. We say, as Nephi predicted, "All is well in Zion." Put in other words, people will say, "Nothing is wrong with our marriage; we're all right. It's nothing really serious." I've noted this attitude to be particularly prevalent among some LDS husbands. They are hesitant either to acknowledge that anything is wrong with their marriages or to do anything about their problems once they are known. But notice what happens: "And thus the devil cheateth their souls, and leadeth them away carefully down into hell." How clever and cunning he is! He takes us by the hand and leads us *carefully* along the path of marital destruction. So sly is he that we often don't know, or won't acknowledge, what is happening to us.

This trend was significantly brought to my attention one time when I was counseling with an LDS woman. She informed me that she had decided to leave her husband. In the next appointment, which was with the husband, I finally said, "Russ, you know your wife is going to leave you if you don't change some things in your marriage right now."

I will never forget his reply: "Dr. Barlow, my wife can't leave me. She's been sealed to me in the temple." Talk about apathy! This man thought he somehow owned his wife. He even stated that she had "been given to him" through the priesthood, and because of that attitude, he felt little or no need to do anything to nurture the relationship. Three months later they were civilly divorced.

The third tactic, flattery, is even more deceiving. Nephi states that "others he flattereth away." (2 Ne. 28:22.) If the first two tactics of anger and pacification don't work, he can usually get us with the third, flattery.

I would dare say that a good many LDS marriages and families have been broken up because of flattery. It may come in one of many forms. It may come through the attention or flattery of a member of the opposite sex. Flattery may be used to get us to believe that certain employment or social or church positions are more important than being a good wife, mother, husband, or father. Or flattery may be used in more subtle ways, even when we are trying to promote righteous causes.

In all honesty, this is one area in which I met the devil, so to speak, on my doorstep. I have a Ph.D. in marriage counseling (an honor of men that sets a person up for flattery), and I write a newspaper column on marriage, teach marriage classes at BYU, conduct marriage seminars, and have appeared often on television to discuss marriage. If one is not careful, such activities can lead to false notions about oneself. I got to the point where I was doing a great deal of traveling on the weekends to do a lot of speaking on marriage. Susan didn't mind—at first. She often went with me. And I was doing the presentations with the genuine interest of trying to help others in their marriages.

The phone would ring, and the conversation would go something like this: "Hello, Dr. Barlow? You spoke in my sister's ward at such and such a place (or I heard you speak at BYU Education Week), and I would like you to come to speak to our group." I would put down the phone, look at my speaking schedule, and then reply, "It doesn't look like I'll be able to do so for the next four months. I'm all booked up." Then the flattery would begin. "Oh, we'll be so disappointed. We looked forward to hearing from you. You are (flattery, flattery)." After so much of it I would start to think, "Yes, I really should go to speak to them. They are saying such kind things about me." So I would give in and somehow find the time to go give the speech.

After several months of this hectic pace, Susan and I began to realize that something could happen to our own marriage. While we were out trying to help others, our own could be hurt. We could be "led carefully" toward the path of marital destruction. Fortunately, we became aware of what was happening in time to take effective measures. I began to turn down many of the invitations to speak, and I was released from some Church callings to devote a greater amount of time to my wife and children. While trying to juggle so many activities, we learned to appreciate Ecclesiastes 3:1: "To

19

every thing there is a season, and a time to every purpose." I sometimes shudder to think how carefully and cunningly, even in the name of righteous causes, we can be duped through flattery into life's many detours. I thought I could keep doing what I was doing with no consequences to my own marriage or family. I learned well what Nephi warned us of: "Wo be unto him that is at ease in Zion! Wo be unto him that crieth: All is well!" (2 Ne. 28:24-25.)

As a Roaring Lion

I don't know if you have ever thought of the devil roaming about in our midst seeking to destroy us. But that is exactly the analogy that Peter uses. In 1 Peter 5:8 he states: "Be sober, be vigilant; because your adversary the devil, as a roaring lion, walketh about, seeking whom he may devour." That is quite vivid imagery! Imagine a roaring lion stalking about our neighborhoods, waiting for the chance to overcome us. That particular verse had recently taken on a new significance for a man in Fort Lauderdale, Florida.

Terry Murphy; his wife, Kathie; and their two sons, Ryan, age 3, and Todd, age 7, moved to a fairly wealthy section of Fort Lauderdale. Terry admits at the time he was quite success oriented. At age 32 he was already doing well in the financial world. But he wanted more. One of his main goals was to own a white Rolls Royce as soon as he could afford it. Terry also confided that at that time he was not particularly religious. Kathie, however, was a devout Christian. He accompanied her and their two boys to church services occasionally, mostly to please Kathie. He was, in his own words, going "through the motions of trying to understand her faith."

But upon moving into the new elite neighborhood, the Murphys discovered something that concerned them. Their neighbor, a man they knew only as "Mr. B," had a real, full-grown lion on a chain in the backyard.

Several months went by with no incident involving Mr.

B's lion. Then one afternoon Terry and Kathie were relaxing by the swimming pool in their backyard. Ryan and Todd were playing on the sidewalk near the front of the house. Suddenly there was a bone-chilling scream from Todd: "Daddy! Daddy! The lion's got Ryan!"

Terry jumped from his lawn chair and ran to the corner of the house. Then he froze in horror at what he saw. The neighbor's lion, obviously unchained and loose, had its jaws clamped on little three-year-old Ryan's neck. Its huge paw was also holding the little boy down. Terry stated he did not know immediately what to do. All he knew was he had to get his son away from the lion.

He ran to the beast and took hold of its jaws. Kathie soon arrived and began to pray that her husband would have the strength to pry the jaws off the neck of their little son. Kathie prayed and Terry pulled. Suddenly the lion's jaws opened, and they pulled their son away. Then Terry called the police.

Soon an ambulance arrived and rushed the young boy to the hospital. The lion's teeth had penetrated Ryan's windpipe, requiring immediate surgery. It was performed successfully, and in two weeks Ryan was released. In three months he had recovered both emotionally and physically from the incident.

How would a father feel when he saw a loved one in the jaws of a lion? Terry Murphy wrote:

> I have changed in many ways. No longer have I a problem with covetousness for material things. The Bible says "Seek ye first the kingdom of God, and His righteousness; and all these things shall be added unto you." (Matthew 6:33.) I have placed Him first in my life, from tithing to giving to others. And still, my family has been abundantly blessed. . . .
>
> I have learned much about evil and how like a lion it can devour us if we are not sober and vigilant. But I have also come to know the One Who stands between us and evil, the One Who gave me the courage and strength to pry open that Lion's jaws. (Murphy, pp. 16-19.)

21

Limits to Satan's Powers

Even though Satan has great power among mankind at the present time, there are limits to his powers and capabilities. Lawrence R. Peterson addressed this topic in the "I Have a Question" column of the *Ensign*. He observed:

> One of the most impressive doctrines found in the Book of Mormon is that Satan's power over a person increases as that person becomes more wicked until eventually the person is "taken captive by the devil" and bound with the "chains of hell." (Alma 12:11.) Satan's method is to influence the thoughts of men, tempting them and enticing them, always working "in the hearts of the children of men." (2 Ne. 28:20.)
>
> But Satan's power is not unrestrained. Joseph Smith taught that Satan has no power over us unless we give it to him. And Nephi explained that the righteousness of a people deprives Satan of his power, "for he hath no power over the hearts of the people, for they dwell in righteousness." (1 Ne. 22:26.)
>
> Between the extremes of Satan's power to captivate and of his utter powerlessness stretches the spectrum of his ability to entice or tempt. As a being of spirit, he works in the realm of spirit, counterbalanced by the Spirit of God. In this way, free agency is preserved, giving us a choice between good and evil. As Lehi taught, "Man could not act for himself save it should be that he was enticed by one or the other." (2 Ne. 2:16.) If Satan entices us to do evil, so the Holy Spirit "entices" us to virtue. (See Mosiah 3:19.) Free agency demands that neither the Holy Spirit nor the evil spirit have power to control the person against his will. (Peterson, Lawrence, pp. 30-31.)

I hope that we may all have enough courage and power to keep ourselves and our loved ones from the "roaring lion." Peter admonishes us to be sober and diligent and to "resist stedfast in the faith" that evil lion. (1 Pet. 5:8-9.) In Doctrine and Covenants 10:5, the Lord advises, "Pray always, that you may come off conqueror; yea, that you may conquer Satan, and that you may escape the hands of the servants of Satan that do uphold his work."

In describing twelve common traps in marriage, I am going to ask LDS married couples to move up to the edge of the ditch, to put on their flak jackets, to "fear" and to stand guard against the adversary. I believe that if we are alert to the dangers to contemporary marriage, we can avoid or overcome them, if we so desire. Unfortunately, too many of us are not taking enough action to reinforce our marriages.

| TRAP 1 |
| THE |
| TIME |
| TRAP |
| |

Time: A measurable period during which an action, process, or condition exists.

THE TIME TRAP: *Spending an inadequate amount of time as a married couple to maintain or improve the marriage.*

O n one occasion Jesus said, "For where your treasure is, there will your heart be also." (Matt. 6:21.) A similar statement might be made about time: we spend time on the things we value. So, by measuring or observing where we spend our time, we can obtain a fairly accurate evaluation of what we value in life.

How many times have we heard and perhaps used the phrase "I don't have time." Sound familiar? We have all heard it, and perhaps we use it often. The truth is, we all have the same amount of time: we have 86,400 seconds, 1,440 minutes, or 24 hours a day; 168 hours a week. Interestingly, the human tendency is that we find time to do the things we want to do, the things we value.

Most of us have been reminded often that we should spend time with our children. LDS Homefront messages on television remind us that we should spend time with our children and family. As a father, I, too, struggle with the issue of spending enough time with my children.

I think most of us are somewhat sensitive to the issue of time with children. I feel, however, that we are often less sensitive to the issue of time with a spouse. There must be time not only to strengthen bonds with children, but also time to strengthen bonds with a husband or wife.

We are sometimes trapped into thinking that the time spent in building families will also build marriages. It will not. Building a marriage often requires different activities . . . and time apart from the children. Last summer, for instance, we took our children to Lagoon, a recreational park north of Salt Lake City. It was a hot July afternoon, and the kids spilled punch on the car seat on the way there. Two got sick on the rides, and the car radiator overheated on the way home. In addition, we all got sunburned during the day. But all the children said it was a good family outing. We, the parents, however, were exhausted at the end of the day. It should come as no surprise that, while our trip to Lagoon was a good family outing, it was not highly romantic. Susan and I have other needs as husband and wife that are not met following kids around a recreation park. We have learned that time together as husband and wife is not only desirable but absolutely essential to the well-being of both our marriage and the family.

As I discuss this observation with husbands and wives, the question often arises as to what counts as "time with spouse." Some husbands claim that watching television together counts as time together. Others believe that the periods both are puttering around in the house, eating meals, or even sleeping is time together. Still others believe that any family outing meets the needs of the marriage and counts as time with the spouse.

What is time together as husband and wife? It could be a variety of things or activities, but I believe the time that counts most between husband and wife is the time when there are no distractions such as children, television, newspapers, or phone calls. In addition, I believe the married couple should be isolated to the point that they can talk to each other, about each other, on the deeper levels of ideas, emotions, and feelings, rather than about the routines of things and people. (See "Trap 5: The Talk Trap.")

With this new definition of time together as husband and wife, let's take the Time Test. Where do we spend our time? Get out a blank sheet of paper and jot down some numbers.

The Time Test

There are 168 hours in a week. In the spaces in the following chart determine approximately *how many hours* of each week you presently devote to each area. Then determine approximately *what percentage of time* of each week is spent in each category. (Helpful hint: 17 hours equals about 10 percent of a week.)

27

Category I	Hours (Weekly)	Percent (Weekly)
Necessary Activities		
Sleeping	_____	_____
Job/occupation	_____	_____
Household management	_____	_____
Eating	_____	_____
Child care	_____	_____
Other: _____	_____	_____
Other: _____	_____	_____
Subtotals:	_____	_____

Category II	Hours (Weekly)	Percent (Weekly)
Individual and Recreational Activities		
Sports/hobbies	_____	_____
Exercise/health care	_____	_____
Education/study	_____	_____
Church/community	_____	_____
Reading	_____	_____
Television	_____	_____
Other: _____	_____	_____
Other: _____	_____	_____
Other: _____	_____	_____
Subtotal:	_____	_____

Category III	Hours (Weekly)	Percent (Weekly)
Family Activities		
Extended family	_____	_____
Family and friends	_____	_____

Children/children and spouse		
Subtotal:		

Category IV	Hours (Weekly)	Percent (Weekly)
Couple Activities		
Spouse		
Subtotal:		
GRAND TOTALS:	168	100%

How did you do? What did you learn from the Time Test? Let me make a few observations. Most people spend approximately 80 percent of their time in Category I and 15 percent in Category II. But what about Category III, Family Activities, and more importantly, Category IV, Couple Activities?

I believe from numerous observations that many married couples spend about two to three hours a week, if that many, on marriage maintenance. Percentage wise, that comes out to less than two percent of our time. Frankly, I don't think that is enough. Some couples just have their weekly "dates," which are often less than spontaneous, and on occasion, when things appear to be very tense, a night or two away. In a moment of marital crisis, they may also take a vacation, sort of a second honeymoon, to see if they can repair a badly damaged relationship. Sometimes it helps. Sometimes it doesn't.

The irony to me is how much lip service we pay to marriage. It is supposed to be central to our lives, yet we allow less than two percent of our time, if that much, for what is supposed to be the most important human relationship in our lives.

Marriage Maintenance

One Saturday I took our automobile to be serviced. While waiting I read an interesting article in one of the magazines in the waiting room. It was titled "A Car's Worst Enemy." A recent survey of more than 5,000 four-year-old cars indicated

29

that eight percent had never had an oil change, and eleven percent had never had an oil filter replaced. And over twenty percent of the cars still had their original antifreeze, air filters, and spark plugs. What was the conclusion? A car's worst enemy may be its owner.

The same article noted a study by the American Automobile Association club of Maryland that indicated similar trends. Of 9,000 cars tested in their state, twenty-nine percent had faulty tires and needed carburetor adjustments. About twenty-seven percent needed major tuning. Another twenty percent needed fan belts and heater hoses replaced, and seventeen percent had ignition problems. The battery water and radiator coolant were low in sixteen percent of the cars examined. Another fourteen percent needed new air filters, twelve percent had low transmission fluid, eleven percent had low electrical systems output, and eight percent needed the PCV system repaired.

The article suggested that Americans love their cars, drive them millions of miles each year, and have high expectations of performance. And the irony is that many do not have even routine maintenance performed on their automobiles. The article hit close to home. A year earlier I almost ruined a $400 transmission by failing to change the transmission fluid, but I caught the error in time at a cost of only $30.

As I glanced up from the magazine to see how they were doing on my car, I noticed a sign on the wall. It stated, "It is easier to change oil than to change engines!" Later, while driving home, I reflected on how careless we become with the maintenance of our cars. I couldn't help but wonder if that didn't suggest some message about the maintenance of our marriages. Are we, as married couples, also our own worst enemies?

When we marry, most of us have high expectations of ourselves and our marriage partners. As the months and then the years go by, we continue to demand and expect much of ourselves and our marriages. Over the years, though, the constant grind of routines and many other daily demands begin to wear us down. Expectations are not always met, and we lose patience. Tempers flare and nerves wear thin. Why? Because we may be constantly drawing from a marriage relationship without making many major investments back into it. We often fail to perform even routine maintenance.

What have you done lately to maintain not so much your automobile but your marriage? We often talk of having periodic "dates," which many husbands think is sufficient. It may not be. Sometimes that is like adding a teaspoon of oil to a crankcase when the car is out of oil. It may take more. Marriage maintenance, I believe, may require more daily attention. It may take twenty minutes a day of private conversation WOCOTV (without children or television). It may take lots of hugs and kisses and some fine tuning of the sexual relationship.

Marriage maintenance may require more frequent verbal expressions of love. It may take occasional gifts and, yes, even the periodic "date" or night out. It may mean a second honeymoon overnight at a downtown hotel. And, as finances permit, a vacation just for the two of you. I know all this takes time and money, but a television advertisement for car lubrication also warns, "You can pay a little now, or a lot later." Divorces are not cheap either, financially or emotionally.

It is, indeed, easier to change oil than to change engines. And it may also be easier to change habits than to change spouses. Marriage maintenance may be a better investment than either repair, rehabilitation, or replacement.

How to Get Out of the Time Trap

In my estimation you are caught in the Time Trap if you are spending two percent or less of your time (only two to three hours a week) on marriage maintenance. Some couples may be spending more. Others are spending less, and in some instances no time at all.

If you want to get out of the Time Trap, I suggest you try the 3 Ts Exercise. Rather than wait for a weekend and spend a block of time (two to five hours) on the typical dinner/movie

31

syndrome, spend just twenty minutes a day with your spouse in Time, Talk, and Touch.

For the Time, spend twenty minutes a day talking and listening to your marriage partner. Marriage studies have shown that just a few minutes a day over a period of time will do more to help a marriage than the occasional marathon of several hours. Just twenty minutes a day will help keep Dr. Barlow (and all other marriage counselors) away! Twenty minutes a day adds up to two hours and twenty minutes a week. That will start you off at the two percent mark of marriage maintenance, if you are not already there.

For the Talk part of the 3 Ts Exercise, first look over "Trap 5: The Talk Trap." Try to talk about more personal things such as feelings and ideas rather than the daily routines you experience. Remember to take turns—let one talk and let one listen, and then reverse the situation.

For the Touch, you may want to put your arms around each other, hold hands, or touch in some other way during your twenty minutes together. It is amazing to me that some couples find this difficult if not impossible to do. If you feel uncomfortable with the touch factor, skip it and practice the two Ts: Time and Talk: But remember, if you cannot touch each other often in nonsexual ways, you may be caught in the Touch Trap as well (see "Trap 10: The Touch Trap").

I honestly believe that the 3 Ts Exercise is one of the most effective means of marriage maintenance today. I assign it for the couples enrolled in my marriage enhancement classes and seminars at Brigham Young University. Here are some comments from husbands and wives about the 3 Ts Exercise:

> *Wife:* The phrase "I don't have time" has developed an even stronger meaning during the past few weeks. When first given the 3 Ts assignment, I thought it would be fun . . . and easy. It's just what I'd been looking for—time with my husband alone. At first it was neither easy nor fun. I found out that Bill and I are in the "Time Trap." We both have hectic schedules and see each other only for a few hours at night (besides sleeping). Bill feels that leisure time

is for eating, reading the paper, and watching television. I know he needs these things, but I want him to need me as well. I want to fit into his schedule. It kind of hurts. He says I'm #1 and he loves me dearly, and I believe him. But if he loves me so much, why can't we find twenty minutes a day to talk to each other?

Young bride: Attending school after having been married only a month has been very difficult for me. We've been so busy with our new life that all we really have time to talk about is what our day consisted of and to say a quick "I love you." Taking twenty minutes a day to talk, communicate, and unwind with my husband has really helped. It lets each of us know that even though we are busy all day, we can still take time for our marriage. Without the twenty minutes each day, things tend to build up until they're taken out on the partner.

Husband: I feel very positive about this exercise. We plan to continue using it in our marriage since it will insure us of at least twenty minutes a day when we can openly communicate our feelings to one another without distractions. I believe it will be a great asset to our marriage if we continue to use the 3 Ts Exercise consistently.

Wife: We have started to talk to each other each night for about twenty minutes before we pray. I can't believe the difference it makes in every aspect of our relationship. That's not to say that we don't have conflicts, but even if we do, they are handled differently now. We no longer avoid discussions when the conflicts appear. We are now more relaxed about it all. It feels good.

Husband: When we talked for our twenty minutes, we held hands and felt closer to each other. When we were touching, it helped us take the time more seriously and use it wisely with good heart-to-heart conversation. I'm glad we learned about the 3 Ts Exercise.

Young wife: I appreciate knowing that my husband thinks about me during the day. I had always felt that when we were apart he would be doing "his own thing" with no thought of me. During our twenty minutes he stated he thought of me often while we were apart. That made me feel good. It is important during the 3 Ts Exercise to sit down without any other distractions such as television and phone calls. We have no children yet, so I assumed it would be easy to spend twenty minutes talking together, but it was more difficult than I expected.

Do you have enough time to build or improve your marriage? You have as much time as anyone else. It is just how you choose to use it. Like other living things, a marriage must have time to develop and grow—we must, in other words, "let patience have her perfect work." (James 1:4.)

It was Henry Austin Dobson who wrote:

> Time goes, you say! Ah no!
> Alas, Time stays, *we* go.
> "The Paradox of Time," st. 1

| TRAP 2 |
| THE |
| TRADITION |
| TRAP |

Tradition: The handing down of statements, beliefs, legends, customs, and behavior patterns from generation to generation, especially by word of mouth or by practice.

THE TRADITION TRAP: *The insistence that marriage today must be exactly as it has been in the past.*

T he past holds much that is "virtuous, lovely, or of good report or praiseworthy" (A of F 13), which we should retain and seek after. Paul also admonishes us to "prove all things; hold fast that which is good." (1 Thes. 5:21.) Allow me, however, to give some examples from my own marriage of the disruption of tradition.

If you had been able to visit our house on Christmas Eve the first few years of our marriage, you would have found an interesting situation, particularly after we had our first children. We found we differed in how to celebrate this traditional holiday. In my family we had always opened our gifts from family members on Christmas Eve. I fondly remember exchanging the personal gifts on the night before Christmas and then opening the presents from Santa on Christmas morning.

But Susan's family was different. Only holiday heretics would open gifts before Christmas day (she never said that publicly, but that was how she felt). True believers would save all their gifts to be opened on Christmas morning.

The question of whether gifts should be opened on Christmas Eve or on Christmas Day should not become a national issue. But for us then, it was an issue (though not now since I have become a true believer), and for some time we had many discussions about this particular tradition. When our children became old enough to sense the difference of opinion between their parents, they played on my wife's sympathy by begging to open a present or two on Christmas Eve. They cited Dad's family tradition as the rationale. Luckily, our marriage has survived this particular collision of family traditions.

Another seemingly trivial tradition came with cookie baking. When I was a boy, my mother used to bake chocolate chip cookies every Saturday. Not only that, but she put plump raisins in them to spice them up a bit. I still become nostalgic when I reminisce about my mother's chocolate chip cookies . . . with raisins.

The first summer we were married, Susan decided one

day that she was going to bake some cookies. She asked what kind I liked, and I replied chocolate chip. Later that afternoon she proudly displayed her first batch of chocolate chip cookies for me. And guess what? I was dumb enough to ask, "What happened to the raisins?" Then, to add insult to injury, I stated, "That's how my mother used to bake them."

Susan is not a violent person. She has never struck me, nor I her. But that afternoon she picked up a ripe grape on the table and threw it at me (a subtle form of nonverbal communication). Since she is a good shot, she hit me right on the forehead. Never again have I mentioned my mother's chocolate chip cookies . . . with raisins. And what's more, I didn't get any kind of cookies for a long time after that incident.

Still another collision of family traditions occurred shortly after we were married. In Susan's family her mother and father, Cecil and Alice Day, had an interesting arrangement. Alice did all the cooking, and Cecil did all the dishes! Need I say more? In my family my father helped wash the dishes on occasion, but there was no woman on earth who could wash dishes faster than my mother. When she finished eating, she would start washing dishes. With luck we were through eating by the time she was ready to wash our dishes. Well, guess what our little problem was regarding dish washing after we were married? And a dishwasher hasn't entirely solved the problem. Now we face the question of who will load and unload the dishwasher.

Opening gifts at Christmas, making chocolate chip cookies, and washing dishes may be relatively minor problem areas, but they are examples of how tradition in marriage can produce problems. We become caught in the tradition trap when we insist that marriage must be as it has been in the past. Or, worse yet, when we insist or demand that our marriage must be exactly like that of our parents.

One time I was talking to a young couple who were about to marry. The future bride expressed some misgivings and apprehensions about their future marriage. The young woman had graduated from college and was well established

37

in a financially and personally rewarding career. But she felt that both her fiancé and his family expected her to immediately cease employment after marriage and "settle down" to have a family, as his mother had done. In addition, he and his side of the family questioned whether she should work at all once they were married. The marriage was called off until the prospective bride and groom discussed and finally decided that she could work at her career at some future point in their marriage, even if his mother had not in hers.

Garbage and Tradition

The tradition of how to handle garbage has even become an issue.

Wednesday is an interesting day at our home. It is the day the city sends around the garbage truck to pick up the garbage, and someone has to take it out to the curb. Susan and I were jogging one Tuesday evening, and the thought struck me that perhaps she should now start taking the garbage out on Wednesday morning. So I said, "Susan, have you noticed who has been taking the garbage out during our many years of marriage?"

"Yes," she said, "and that is the way I want it."

We jogged along a little farther, and I said, "Why is it that you seldom take out the garbage?"

"For two simple reasons," she replied. "First, the garbage cans are heavy; and second, I don't like garbage."

I have no real love for garbage either, but still, I thought we could overcome tradition and start sharing the responsibility of getting the garbage cans to the curb on Wednesday morning.

"According to research," I said as I puffed along, "it is now the wife who takes out the garbage most of the time in contemporary marriages."

"Whose research is that?" she asked over her shoulder since she was two steps ahead of me.

I hesitated.

38

"Actually, it's mine," I replied. "As I drive along the streets on the way to the university on Wednesday mornings, I notice that relatively few men take out garbage cans anymore. I am one of the few remaining husbands who still takes out the garbage."

"Research and observations to the contrary, I'd rather not take out the garbage," she said as we stopped to count pulse rates.

So I tried another approach. "You know, Susan, there are many changes today in what we perceive to be husband's work and wife's work. You've heard of blended roles, shared parenting, joint housekeeping, and all that. We've got to become less traditional in our marriage. We can't be bound by those silly traditions that say men must always take out the garbage."

We ran a little more. She didn't say much and I knew she was thinking, which meant that I was knee-deep in trouble.

"You want to do away with tradition, huh?"

"Yes," I replied. "I think it is time for that."

"And you think we should be less traditional in our marriage, do you?"

Again I stated that was what I wanted.

"OK," she said, and she stopped. This time it was not to count pulse rates. "We'll do away with tradition and become more contemporary. I'll start taking the garbage out every other week."

We started jogging again, and I chuckled inside. What a blow for male liberation! But we had not gone five more strides when she continued, "And you start fixing breakfast on Monday, Wednesday, and Friday. Also, you may put the kids to bed on Tuesday, Thursday, and Saturday. On Sunday, we'll flip a coin . . . for equality. Loser both fixes dinner and puts the children to bed."

We jogged on for a few more minutes. No one said anything. This time I was thinking. Maybe taking the garbage out every Wednesday morning was not so bad. There should be fixed roles so everyone knows who is supposed to do what.

Order is essential in everyday life. Tradition does serve some purpose.

I ran a little ahead of Susan. "Where are you going?" she called.

"It's getting dark, and I want to get home early," I turned around and shouted back. "I'm not sure I'll have time to put the garbage cans out in the morning, so I wanted to get it done tonight."

As I quickened my pace she called ahead, "What about breakfast . . . and putting the children to bed?"

I didn't say anything. In fact I didn't even turn around to respond. I just ran home and put out the garbage cans.

Just out of curiosity, who takes out the garbage at your house? And more importantly, who do you think should? How traditional are you in your marriage?

Tarzan and Jane Roles Must Go

Many may not be aware that marriage and our expectations of it have changed dramatically during the past two decades. Some hold tenaciously to traditions of the past, only to find it difficult if not impossible to survive in contemporary times. This doesn't mean that we should give up all traditions from the past. There are many good things previously advocated that we still need today or that can enrich our lives.

Nevertheless, there are some aspects of marriage in the past that are no longer tolerable, particularly for women. This was indicated in a letter I received from a woman who recently divorced her husband. Much of their problem, she stated, was the "Tarzan and Jane" role expectations she and her former husband had of marriage and of each other. She wrote:

> I have been divorced for a year now. Our marriage lasted three years, and we had known each other for several years before we were married. Our problems encompassed the familiar and perhaps the not-so-familiar. Before we were married each of us was independent and self-supporting. We admired those traits in each other and

40

found them attractive. After marriage, however, these qualities became less attractive and led to much anger.

Our built-in stereotyped expectations of husband and wife roles got in the way. We lost sight of who and what we had been to each other as lovers and individuals before we were married. After the marriage, we held each other to rigid expectations of what we thought the other should do or be. I was supposed to be like his mother: a tender of the home fires, the supportive one, the baker of bread, something he knew I wasn't or couldn't be. He, in turn, was to become the fixer of cars, the plumber, and overall handyman.

After our marriage each of us struggled to keep or put the other into the preassigned traditional niche. During that time I think we privately mourned the loss of the period before marriage when our self-imposed demands did not exist—when we just lived our lives and did what needed to be done. Our unrealistic expectations after marriage became a constant source of conflict as we continually negotiated our mutual and exclusive territory. Obviously, we did not survive.

Each time one of us tried to do something on the basis of skill, knowledge, or expertise instead of assigned, traditional roles, the other would be hurt. It was a matter of pride, insecurity, and a fear of losing control over our own lives or selves. When men expect their wives to be their mothers, or women expect husbands to be their fathers, no one wins. Yet we had no other models. The women's movement may have exaggerated this point, but it may have also created the possibility for a healthier life for all, both male and female.

After our marriage I chose to work because I loved my job and was uplifted by it. But even with a joint income of $80,000, I was predestined by gender to be the one to scrub the toilets. We could never get by that in our marriage. With that much income we could have afforded a housekeeper or a semimonthly maid, yet because I was the wife I was genetically ordained to push the vacuum.

We found marriage to be difficult because we were not flexible. The "Tarzan and Jane" stereotypes must give way if we are going to survive marriage at the present time. We cannot go back to the 1950s, 60s, or even 70s—those days are gone forever. And we may continue to destroy each other in marriage until we can learn to live with each other as genuine individuals with more flexible roles for today's marriage.

Is Housework Unmasculine?

If you as the wife have had a difficult time getting your husband to wash the dishes and help a little around the house, as did this woman, I can now tell you why. It is unmasculine—not manly. That is, according to one observer who also happens to be a man.

I really have nothing against Zig Ziglar personally. He is apparently an excellent speaker, and if I remember correctly, he has spoken in Salt Lake City a time or two in some of the motivation seminars. He has also written a best-selling book, *See You at the Top*, that has sold several hundred thousand copies.

His book, published several years ago, was particularly interesting to me because he has some advice on how to be better husbands and wives. But he writes something that concerns me and likely many others. To the wives of America, he wrote: "You do the jobs that are essentially feminine. I'm convinced that a contributing factor in many of our problems today is the lack of a clear distinction between male and female. Men should look, dress, act, think, and talk like men. Women should look, dress, act, think, and talk like women. Any time we have to pause and wonder if it's male or female, that's sad." (Ziglar, p. 143.)

So far, so good. Nothing earth-shattering yet. But now read what he advises:

> I believe under normal conditions the wife should wash dishes and make up the beds. Obviously there are some circumstances which dictate that the loving husband dig in and help. Generally speaking, though, I don't believe it is a good idea for a little boy to see Dad in the dishpan, nor do I believe little girls should consistently see Mom assuming a male role and performing masculine chores. . . . Let the

42

little boy see the male role and he will grow up to be a man with a natural affection for the opposite sex. (Ziglar, pp. 143-44.)

There you have it—with the implication that the world in general and marriages in specific are in such a mess because men have started washing the dishes. Or, as little boys, their psyches were damaged because they peered in the kitchen late one evening and caught dad helping mother. I haven't seen any of the more recent publications of *See You at the Top*, but I hope that the previous passage, or at least the opinion, has been omitted.

The Census Bureau recently reported that among 26.3 million married couples in the United States, 62 percent have two incomes from both spouses working. In 1960, only 40 percent of the married couples were "two-paycheck marriages," but by 1970 the figure had risen to 50 percent. It is anticipated that by 1990, 70 percent of the couples will have both husband and wife earning an income, and by 2000 A.D., the turn of the century, 80 percent or more of the married couples will have marriages in which both partners work. It has become clear that the traditional division of household tasks is changing. Although the husband may initially resist, once he has become accustomed to the economic benefits of two paychecks, he is likely to be open to negotiation and make concessions rather than lose his wife's earnings.

In adapting to the wife's employment, husbands sometimes feel that their self-esteem is threatened—they may feel embarrassment, guilt, or apprehension associated with the wife's employment or feel that their importance to the marriage is lessened. For wives, the problem oftentimes is getting the husbands to share the housework. At first, the wife may shift some of her duties onto older children or avoid work by using frozen foods, having fewer dinner parties, or simply cleaning the house less often. But once it becomes obvious that she is in the working world for good, she is likely to urge her husband to pitch in with the housework.

Generally, better-educated men do more housework than those with less schooling. Also, the higher a wife's earnings, the more likely it is that her husband will help out with the housework. However, men generally do less around the house if the husband's pay greatly exceeds the wife's. Certainly there is nothing to support Zig Ziglar's premise that a husband will never "make it to the top" if he starts helping his wife with the dishes.

The Peter Pan Syndrome

Dr. Dan Kiley, a psychologist, has written an interesting book titled *The Peter Pan Syndrome—Men Who Have Never Grown Up*. We all remember the story of the happy-go-lucky Peter Pan, who symbolizes the essence of youthfulness in his experiences with Captain Hook. As Peter Pan cavorts with Tinkerbell and captures the ship *Jolly Roger*, he awakens the child in all of us. We are drawn to him and allow ourselves to be nourished by his exuberant youth.

But according to Dr. Kiley, there is another side of the classic character created by J. M. Barrie. Kiley states: "Have you stopped to consider why Peter wanted to stay young? Sure, it's tough to grow up, but Peter Pan avoided it vehemently. What made him reject all things adult? What was he really after? Is it as simple as it sounded? Was not Peter's desire to stay young actually a militant refusal to grow up? If so, what was his problem? Or problems?" (Kiley, p. 23.)

From this well-known story, Kiley draws the analogy between contemporary adult males who will not grow up and the youthful Peter Pan—hence the term *Peter Pan syndrome*. What are some of its characteristics? According to the psychologist there are seven: irresponsibility, anxiety, loneliness, sex role conflict, narcissism, chauvinism, and social impotence.

Dr. Kiley also claims that there are two kinds of women who interact with men who won't grow up. He calls them "Wendys" and "Tinkers" (from Tinkerbell). He notes that one is willing to take the back seat and assume the role of a protective mother figure:

> She is insecure herself, and the victim's dependency makes her feel needed. It even gives her a distorted sense of strength. Her sex with the PPS [Peter Pan syndrome] victim is ritualistic and predictable; it's also very quickly over with. She doesn't recognize that the victim is immature, and she persuades herself to believe that his problems are normal. She sticks with this mate, figuring her love life will improve. It doesn't. I call this type of woman a "Wendy."
>
> The other type of woman wants spontaneity, growth, and mutual adaptation in her relationship with a man. She recognizes the PPS victim's immaturity but is drawn to his devil-may-care attitude. She, too, figures the guy will outgrow some of his behavior. . . . I call this woman a "Tinker." (Kiley, pp. 216-17.)

If you are a woman and think you are married to a "Peter Pan," Dr. Kiley first suggests that you determine whether or not you are a Wendy or a Tinker. If you are the former, you should stop doing Wendy-like things. Kiley has an interesting section titled "On Becoming a Tinker" with several suggestions on what to stop and to start doing to make your husband less dependent on you.

But I have a simpler suggestion. Ask your husband if he is a Peter Pan who is, among other things, irresponsible, chauvinistic, and overly dependent on women. If he says no, ask him to prove it. Ask him to take over running the house for a few days while you take a breather. If he agrees, fine. Hand him your apron and find your favorite book. But if he refuses to take over, you might buy him a copy of Dr. Dan Kiley's book, *The Peter Pan Syndrome*. And if he asks why you did it, just tell him it was the Tinkerbell coming out in you.

Marriage, What Kind for You?

Housework is one obvious example of tradition and change in contemporary marriage. But there are several other changes that have and are occurring that could harm our marriages if we are not aware of them. Contemporary marriage has significantly changed from the past.

In his book *Close Companions*, Dr. David Mace, a well-known marriage counselor and educator, describes what he calls "The Great Transition." He observes:

> Imagine a human community, long settled in a narrow valley overshadowed by towering mountains. Life for those people has not been easy; but they have managed to survive, and they feel secure in their simple dwellings.
>
> Now, word has come from an exploring party that they have discovered much better land on the other side of the mountain. They speak of fertile plains, abundant pastures, dense forests, and broad rivers. A new and better life beckons.
>
> The migration begins. The bolder spirits go first. Then others follow. Some hesitate, then decide, pack, and set off. Now there are scattered parties on the move, taking various routes. Some go straight over the mountains, others take the longer but less arduous way round. A few grow weary of the journey and establish settlements along the route. Some even turn back.
>
> This provides a fair picture of our cultural transition from the traditional to the companionship marriage. Families everywhere are on the move. Some have already reached the new country; some lag far behind; some are en route, struggling with unanticipated difficulties, exploring new trails and finding they lead nowhere. (Mace, *Close*, p. 50.)

What is the new companionship marriage of which Dr. Mace speaks? How does it differ from the traditional marriage of the past? I believe Dr. Mace has identified better than anyone else the major differences between marriages of the past and marriages of the present. The following chart lists ten of these major differences (Mace, *Close*, p.16):

Traditional Marriage	Our Marriage?	Companionship Marriage
One-vote system—husband makes all major decisions		Two-vote system—decisions jointly made by husband and wife
Fixed roles—husband's and wife's roles clearly differentiated by gender		Fluid roles—roles based on personal choice and competence with little emphasis on gender difference
Husband provider—wife homemaker		Flexible division of provider and homemaker functions
Husband initiates sex—wife complies		Sex initiated by either husband or wife
Basic concept—marriage a hierarchy		Basic concept—marriage an equal partnership
Issues settled with reference to legalistic principles and rules		Issues settled with reference to personal and interpersonal needs
Wife close to children—husband disciplinarian and authority figure		Husband and wife both close to children, both represent authority
Husband assumes role of religious head of family		Religious functions of family shared by husband and wife
Further education important for husband, not for wife		Further education equally important for both
Husband's vocation decides family residence		Family residence takes account of both husband's and wife's vocations

Of these marital trends, Dr. Mace further notes:

> The difference between the old marriage pattern and the new is very clear. The first conforms to a rigid system, which provides ready-made answers to most questions that are likely to arise. The couple don't have to struggle with differences; and they don't have to be much involved in each other's inner thoughts and feelings. The second pattern, by contrast, involves husband and wife in a continuing series of interpersonal interactions and is virtually unworkable unless they can establish the kind of flexible relationship that only companionship makes possible.
>
> The emergence of the companionship marriage was inevitable, and it represents a transition process arising out of a revolt against the rigidities of traditional marriage, in an increasingly open democratic culture. The struggle is epitomized in two highly significant words: *Love* and *Equality*. (Mace, *Close*, pp. 15-16.)

Latter-day Saints, along with others, will likely be interested in Dr. Mace's observations. As I review the characteristics of the two types of marriage, I believe Latter-day Saint couples will find themselves somewhere between the two. Many Church members believe, for example, that (1) the husband should assume the role of religious head of his family, (2) marriage should be a hierarchy (e.g., man "presides" over wife and family), and (3) the husband should be the primary provider and the wife the primary homemaker. On the other hand, many Latter-day Saints believe that (1) marriage should be a two-vote system in which decisions are jointly made by husband and wife, (2) the husband and the wife both should be close to their children and represent authority, and (3) further education is equally important to both spouses. On other issues, we are either uncertain, in a state of transition, or our cultural biases have become confused with our religious practices.

It is obvious to me, however, that we, like others, are undergoing change in our perceptions about marriage. Some Latter-day Saints have suggested to me that the so-called "traditional marriage" is the Latter-day Saint marriage. A few older couples have even gone so far as to suggest that the traditional marriage (all ten characteristics) is the celestial marriage. I hardly think so. In many of our church meetings we may decry the departure from "traditional marriage and family life," but after reviewing the marriage of the past in the United States, many changes are obviously warranted and even welcomed, particularly from a woman's point of view.

Traditional marriage of the past (which originated separate and apart from LDS practice or doctrine) heavily favored the male. It is little wonder, then, that as society became more democratic, some changes in marriage would likely occur. They have, indeed, and though some married couples are still in the valley avoiding the changes, others are struggling up the mountainside, and a few have arrived. Perhaps some things should remain as they are, but other changes should be welcomed. Each couple must decide.

Base Camps and Mountain Peaks

Several people have suggested that I read M. Scott Peck's book *The Road Less Traveled*, so I finally bought a copy and am glad I did. It is an exceptional book written by a very sensitive psychiatrist. The intriguing aspect of this book is its emphasis on building love and developing spiritual growth in today's society. The author is concerned about marital disruption and the number of divorces in the United States. He also gives his insights into what marriages will need in order to survive in these contemporary times. In particular, he makes an interesting comparison between marriage and mountain climbing:

> When dealing with couples my wife and I draw the analogy between marriage and a base camp for mountain climbing. If one wants to climb mountains one must have a good base camp, a place where there are shelter and provisions, where one may receive nurture and rest before one ventures forth again to seek another summit. Successful mountain climbers know that they must spend at least as much time, if not more, in tending to their base camp as

they actually do in climbing mountains, for their survival is dependent upon their seeing to it that their base camp is sturdily constructed and well stocked.

A common and traditionally masculine marital problem is created by the husband who, once he is married, devotes all his energies to climbing mountains and none to tending to his marriage, or base camp, expecting it to be there in perfect order whenever he chooses to return to it for rest and recreation. . . . Sooner or later he returns to find his untended base camp a shambles, his neglected wife having been hospitalized for a nervous breakdown, having run off with another man, or in some other way having renounced her job as camp caretaker.

An equally common and traditionally feminine marital problem is created by the wife, who, once she is married, feels that the goal of her life has been achieved. To her the base camp is the peak. She cannot understand or empathize with her husband's need for achievements and experiences beyond the marriage and reacts to them with jealousy and never-ending demands that he devote increasingly more energy to the home. . . . [This] creates a relationship that is suffocating and stultifying, from which the husband, feeling trapped and limited, may likely flee in a moment of "mid-life crisis."

The only ideal resolution [is] marriage as a truly cooperative institution, requiring great mutual contributions and care, time and energy, but existing for the primary purpose of nurturing each of the participants for individual journeys toward his or her own individual peaks of spiritual growth. Male and female both must tend the hearth and both must venture forth. (Peck, pp. 167-68.)

Once I was giving a marriage seminar in Garden Grove, California. At the conclusion of my seminar I related Dr. Peck's base-camp-and-mountain-peak analogy. When the seminar was over, a couple came up to talk to me. Both were professional mountain climbers, and they had particularly appreciated Dr. Peck's insights. Then they made an interesting observation. Mountain climbers can scale larger mountains, they observed, if they do it with a partner. Because they are joined together with a rope, mountain climbers can help pull each other up when they tire as they climb, and mountain climbers can cushion the fall if a partner slips. These are obvious advantages to climbing mountains with a partner instead of doing it alone. Both thereby derive the benefit of the climb and the view of the summit.

Do you agree with Dr. Peck's analysis of contemporary marriage and his comparison to mountain climbing? He suggests that husbands need to devote more time and attention to the base camp and that wives need to scale more mountain peaks if marriages are not only to survive but also to thrive in these modern times.

Using Dr. Peck's analogy, let us add one last thought. Latter-day Saint husbands and wives should also remember and realize that "no success in mountain climbing can compensate for failure in the base camp."

Change

One of the games we frequently played as children was "Three Wishes," in which we could wish for any three things we wanted. Even as adults we continue to wish for things in life, including wishing for improved marriages.

Wishing or hoping for a better marriage is beneficial in that the couple recognizes the need for change. There are many married couples, however, who are insensitive to the need for an improved relationship. Furthermore, wishing or hoping for any changes may be counterproductive if that is all one does. One of the great myths regarding marriage is that it will improve spontaneously or automatically with little or no effort. Sooner or later we have to confront the reality that hoping isn't coping.

Many marriage partners often desire improved relationships in their marriage, but their expectations aren't always attained. This is frequently because they accomplish nothing constructive to bring about improvement, even though they both know and wish something could be done.

Following are a few suggestions and observations about making change:

1. Confront the reality that changes need to be made not only in thinking but also in behavior. You should not only desire change but also be willing to do something to bring it about.

2. Before presenting your list of demands of desired changes to your spouse, it is usually more helpful to make a list of (a) what you have done, or not done, to contribute to the less-than-desirable marriage, and (b) what you are willing to do in the future to contribute to a better marriage. You can best start on those areas you can control—and those areas are in yourself. By demonstrating your willingness to change and the sincerity of your intentions, you have a better chance of soliciting a similar response from your spouse.

3. Give your impaired marriage adequate time for improvement. Don't expect immediate success in your endeavors. Negative personality traits and undesirable behavior patterns evolve over time and will not likely disappear overnight. One of my colleagues has observed that, when people seek changes in relationships, things often get worse before they get better. Such a development is typically short-lived, however. If people desire to change, are persistent in their efforts, and have ample time to make the change, they will succeed. In essence, old dogs can, in time, learn new tricks.

4. Many married couples seek for and achieve improved relationships without outside help. On occasion, however, it may be necessary to seek help from competent sources. Assistance for working through marital problems is often best found in those who are not emotionally involved in the marriage, which excludes most neighbors, friends, and relatives. It is also wise to seek help from those who have had some training in dealing with marital problems. Competent marriage and family counselors are available in most communities. In addition, religious leaders, mental health workers, and those in the medical and legal professions can also render valuable assistance or make referrals. (See also the last chapter, "Seeking Additional Help.")

Actively seeking to improve marital relationships rather than merely wishing they would get better takes involvement, work, and effort. Ultimately, however, such endeavors are much more satisfying and fulfilling than hoping and waiting for improvements. Perhaps marriage would be more meaningful if we made a diligent effort to do less hoping and more coping in our marital interaction.

How to Get Out of the Tradition Trap

In my opinion, you are in the Tradition Trap if you insist that (1) your marriage now must be exactly as it has been in the past; (2) your marriage must be exactly like that of your parents, relatives, or friends; or (3) your marriage has most of the characteristics of the traditional marriage. To get out of the trap, you must change your marriage relationship and attitudes toward marriage. To do so, you may need to start by changing the way you behave or act toward each other. Look over and then practice the "Showing-Love-by-Deeds Exercise" included at the end of "Trap 4: The Tenderness Trap."

Controlled and constructive change is conducive to a stable marriage. Only living things grow and change. How about your marriage? What changes might you and your spouse try to initiate in your marriage during the next few months? After the areas have been identified, let the reformation begin with you!

TRAP 3

THE

TOGETHERNESS

TRAP

Togetherness: The quality, state, or condition of being together or in union,
proximity, or contact; warm fellowship,
as among members of a family.

THE TOGETHERNESS TRAP: *Having either too
little or too much identity and bonding as a married
couple.*

M ost people think of togetherness as spending time with each other each day, but I will never forget the moment I realized that there is more to "togetherness" than just being in each other's presence. Susan and I had just sat down to reevaluate our marriage. Nothing was really wrong at the time—we just wanted to improve. So we decided we would both jot down on paper a few things we could work on, and then we would share lists. I wrote down one or two ideas that were not that earthshaking, something like "listen more intently when the other is talking" and "help each other with tasks without being asked."

I noticed she was very thoughtful with her writing before she finally completed her list. Then we traded. Imagine my shock when I saw at the top of her list, "Spend more time with me." I was somewhat taken aback by her request and was a little alarmed. I thought I was spending adequate time with her. So we had a very interesting discussion about time and togetherness.

I conveyed to Susan that I thought we did spend time together, and she agreed. "But," she said, "sometimes you're not all here when you're supposed to be. You're physically present but psychologically absent." I began to see what she was getting at, especially after she gave me two examples:

"When we go shopping I like to walk with you down the street or in the mall. But I'm often looking in a window at something, and you are over playing in the gutter or talking to someone else. And when we go to church, supposedly together, you sit on one end of the bench, I on the other, and our seven children all in between. Somehow I don't feel very close to you at the time. When we go to church, I want to sit by you. And I want you to hold my hand during the service."

I told my wife that sometimes when our family goes to church I feel like Snow White trying to monitor the seven dwarfs. I agreed to sit by her, but holding hands in church? I indicated that we were also supposed to listen to the sermons during the service. Susan suggested that if I practiced and had real concentration, perhaps I could do both at the same time. It might be difficult, but she felt I could do it. Now I struggle with my children each Sunday to see who is going to sit by their mother. In addition, I have found I can listen and hold my wife's hand simultaneously. Old dogs can, indeed, learn new tricks.

The trap we sometimes get into is believing that when we are in our spouses' presence, we are "together." That is obviously not always the case. Remember, we can sometimes be physically present and psychologically absent. We should strive for both physical and psychological presence—when we are there, we should be there!

Too Little Togetherness

I once had the opportunity to talk to two LDS missionaries. They had been assigned to be companions for several weeks, but they were not getting along. They wanted to write to the mission president to request a change in companions or a transfer—sort of a missionary companion divorce. The more I talked to the two young elders, the more it became evident to me that they were companions by assignment only. Even though they had been together for several weeks, they scarcely knew each other. During the few weeks they yet had together, I suggested they spend at least thirty minutes a day talking to each other, about each other, and share part of their lives and their feelings about missionary work.

Later, on the day the transfers came, I saw the missionaries again. I asked them individually how they felt about each other as companions. They both acknowledged that no miracles had occurred, but since taking at least a half hour a day to share part of themselves with each other, they had, in their own words, "grown closer" to each other. I think the missionary analogy is appropriate to marriage. Some of us are companions by definition and identity only. We live, eat, and work in close proximity, yet we are not very close. It may be that we have had a wedding but not yet experienced a marriage.

One time I was counseling with a frustrated LDS wife

whose husband was a workaholic physician. He spent twelve to fourteen hours minimum a day at his work six and sometimes seven days a week. Subsequently, his wife was left home to rear the children and manage the house virtually alone. Home for him had become a convenient service station where he went to get refueled and recharged. Then he took off again.

His wife had become extremely frustrated and hostile because of the situation. When her husband was home, he had little if anything to do with their children. She couldn't remember him ever changing a diaper or getting up even once at night when a baby or some other child cried. I asked the woman if they ever went out alone together. She said they did, but it was what she called a "church date." He did it, she said, because their bishop and stake president suggested all brethren take their wives out periodically. She felt it was sort of glorified welfare work. She also believed that the infrequent outings helped ease his guilt about being an absentee father and husband even though he lived at home. The "dates," as she described them, were routine dining and movies.

I asked her if they ever took the time to talk to each other and share their lives and feelings. She began to cry. She said she had indicated to him that she would like to discuss her feelings, but he had just told her to "straighten up" because her emotional state, to him, indicated a lack of discipline and control. If things did not improve, he suggested some medication to calm her down.

This marriage, to me, was a classic case of a husband and wife spending time together, though emotionally and psychologically they were as distant as if they lived hundreds of miles apart. Physical presence in no way assures emotional closeness, and it is my observation that a psychological separation always precedes a physical or literal divorce.

Togetherness, then, might be redefined as the emotional bonding marriage partners have toward each other. Too little togetherness, so defined, is a major problem in marriage.

Too Much Togetherness

The irony about togetherness is that it is a double trap. The one side of the trap is having too little togetherness—a lack of bonding or couple identity. The other equally devastating side of the trap is that we can become too close, too bound together in our marriage.

Too much togetherness can be destructive. Sometimes a husband and wife become like two porcupines in a small cage—both need more room and space to function. On this topic, Elder Hugh W. Pinnock, member of the First Quorum of the Seventy, has cautioned LDS couples against smothering each other with excessive restrictions. He noted:

> A loving wife of many years shared with me one of the secrets of her beautiful marriage. She told me, "It is my duty to maintain an atmosphere in our home in which my husband can reach his full potential. And you know, he is a busy father, bishop, and businessman. In turn, he helps me reach my potential."
>
> With her encouragement, he was an outstanding bishop. She later served as a counselor in two auxiliary presidencies and then as president of the stake Relief Society. She had her own room where she sewed, painted, and wrote beautiful poetry. He felt comfortable in going fishing, doing some painting himself, and growing in ways that interested him. Neither of these marriage partners was being smothered by a selfish mate. Both respected the other's needs and goals.
>
> The most fulfilling of all marriages seem to be those in which the husband and wife together commit their love to the Savior's keeping. They are interested in each other, and yet set each other free to grow and mature, to take on new challenges and to pursue new interests. Of course, this freedom is *not* the freedom to flirt with another. Jealousy is a subtle form of bondage and is one of the most smothering of human passions.
>
> Husbands and wives who fear the loss of a partner's love weaken their relationship by holding on too tightly. A husband who thinks to himself, "I won't let her out of my sight," is actually expressing a fear that might push her

away. Husbands and wives should allow each other room for personal growth and expression. When both marriage partners are able to develop their talents and interests, the marriage is less likely to suffer from boredom and narrowness. (Pinnock, p. 35.)

Quite often the wives are the ones who have little identity apart from husband, house, and children. If they run their homes as service station models, they can wear themselves out or lose their sense of identity if they are not being nurtured while nurturing others. On occasion, wives and mothers need to pursue some additional activities.

One weekend not long ago was interesting for me and a lot of other husbands and fathers in our neighborhood. The reason was that the women in our ward went for an overnight trip together up in a canyon at a camp called Edenbrook. While they were gone, we husbands had to take over all the responsibilities of running the homes and taking care of the children. By the time the women had left, all the food stores in the area were probably sold out of frozen pizza and root beer. Seriously, I think it is appropriate that women do take a little time off together, but I have a friend who disagrees.

He and I were talking about the trip the women were taking, and during our conversation I told him tongue-in-cheek of my plight and the two-day pizza party my children had planned. I explained in a little more detail about the outing and said that Susan looked forward to going.

My friend was quiet for a few moments and then asked, "But what does it really signify when wives and mothers 'have to get away'?"

"Nothing, really," I replied. "To me it is a group of women going on an overnight trip." I didn't see any hidden symbolism in the outing.

He then went on to express concern about all the current attention drawn to the individual, for the need to "get away," as it were, from family and friends, even children and spouses. As evidence, he cited some contemporary beer commercials on television. Several depict a group of men late at night on the beach, or in the mountains, sitting around the campfire, together, and drinking beer. Then the announcer states, "It doesn't get any better than this."

Such advertisements, my friend suggested, are antifamily and undermine the importance of family life. Meaningful experiences, he went on, should be had with family members, not "away" with others.

Obviously my friend disapproved of the women in our neighborhood going up to the church camp overnight. And while we were talking of life's events and symbolism, how could I tell him that they were actually going away . . . to Eden(brook)! I returned home and shared my friend's thoughts with Susan. She said it was a good philosophy but not too practical, indicating she still needed a day or two away.

Why do wives and mothers need time away from husbands and home for a while? Perhaps poet Carol Lynn Pearson has expressed it best. In the preface of her book *The Flight and the Nest*, she has the following poem (Pearson, p. v):

On Nest Building

Mud is not bad for nest building.
Mud and sticks
And a fallen feather or two will do
And require no reaching.
I could rest there, with my tiny ones,
Sound for the season, at least.

But—
If I may fly awhile—
If I may cut through a sunset going out
And a rainbow coming back,
Color upon color sealed in my eyes—
If I may have the unboundaried skies
For my study,
Clouds, cities, rivers for my rooms—
If I may search the centuries
For melody and meaning—
If I may try for the sun—

61

> I shall come back
> Bearing such beauties
> Gleaned from God's and man's very best.
> I shall come filled.
> And then—
> Oh, the nest that I can build!

Susan and her associates enjoyed the trip. But we were all pleased when they came back . . . from Eden.

Even Lovers Need Time Away

I had a conversation not long ago with a young husband who called late one night and got me out of bed. He wanted to talk, so I yawned and agreed to listen. The new groom was upset because his wife of seven months was going home to visit her parents for two weeks.

"How can she stand to be away from me that long?" he asked. The longer he talked, the more I knew why. His wife needed a little time away from the marriage. They were too close and their lives too meshed—a common problem for newlyweds.

I tried to convince the young man that a few days away from each other were not necessarily harmful, and could, in fact, contribute to a better marriage. Everyone, including lovers, needs a little time away.

The thought of spending time away from loved ones is not new. The ancient Hebrew family understood the concept as expressed in Ecclesiastes 3:1-8 where it states there is a season and a time for every purpose: "a time to embrace, and a time to refrain from embracing."

Several years ago Kahlil Gibran also wrote:

> Give your hearts, but not into each other's keeping.
> For only the hand of Life can contain your hearts.
> And stand together yet not too near together:
> For the pillars of the temple stand apart,
> And the oak tree and the cypress grow not in
>   each other's shadow.
>   (Gibran, pp. 15-16.)

Dr. M. Scott Peck, in his book *The Road Less Traveled*, has a whole chapter titled "Love Is Separateness." He writes:

> The genuine lover always perceives the beloved as someone who has a totally separate identity. Moreover, the genuine lover always respects and even encourages this separateness and the unique individuality of the beloved. Failure to perceive and respect this separateness is extremely common, however, and the cause of much mental illness and unnecessary suffering. . . .
>
> Not too long ago in a couples group I heard one of the members state that "the purpose and function" of his wife was to keep their house neat and him well fed. I was aghast at what seemed to me his painfully blatant male chauvinism. I thought I might demonstrate this to him by asking the members of the group to state how they perceived the purpose and function of their spouses. To my horror the six others, male and female alike, gave very similar answers. All of them defined the purpose and function of their husbands or wives in reference to themselves; all of them failed to perceive that their mates might have an existence basically separate from their own or any kind of destiny apart from their marriage. . . .
>
> I have come to realize that it is the separateness of the [marriage] partners that enriches the union. Great marriages cannot be constructed by individuals who are terrified by their basic aloneness. . . . Genuine love not only respects the individuality of the other but actually seeks to cultivate it. (Peck, pp. 161, 166, 168.)

Recognizing the Togetherness Trap

The togetherness trap is quite simple. You have either too little or too much identity and bonding as a married couple, and emotionally you are either too close or too distant from each other. Striking a balance, however, is sometimes difficult to accomplish.

How do you know where you are? Asking each other how you feel on this topic may help. Recognize, too, that not only do individual marriages differ, but couples change as they experience the seasons of life. At some point in their lifetimes they may desire more togetherness, and at other points, less identity and bonding with their marriage partners. Communicating by asking what the other person needs and feels is one way to find out.

Another way to find out and measure not only marital cohesion but also marital adaptability is by taking the MACES III test.

In the previous chapter we talked about tradition and the need for change or adaptability. In this chapter we have talked about togetherness and the need for a balance in marital cohesion. Dr. David Olson and associates at the University of Minnesota have put together a short test to help married couples examine the two variables of adaptability and cohesion in their marriage. The test is called the MACES III (Marital Adaptability and Cohesion Evaluation Scale).

The following 1985 version is the third version of the test. It can be quickly administered and scored. Using the two variables, they have found there are sixteen types of marriage. Which one do you have? Which one do you desire?

MARRIAGE WELLNESS SCALE—
MACES III

Instructions

Listed below are twenty questions regarding your marriage now (Part I) and twenty questions pertaining to how you would like your marriage to be (Part II).

1. On the line next to the question, mark 1, 2, 3, 4, or 5 according to the scale provided. (For example, on question #12, "We jointly make the decisions in our marriage," if your response is "Once in a While," you would write the number 2 on the line.)
2. Answer all forty questions in this manner.

1	2	3	4	5
Almost Never	Once in a While	Sometimes	Frequently	Almost Always

PART I

Your Marriage As It Is Now

_____ 1. We ask each other for help.
_____ 2. When problems arise, we compromise.
_____ 3. We approve of each other's friends.
_____ 4. We are flexible in how we handle our differences.
_____ 5. We like to do things with each other.
_____ 6. Different persons act as leaders in our marriage.
_____ 7. We feel closer to each other than to people outside our family.
_____ 8. We change our way of handling tasks.
_____ 9. We like to spend free time with each other.
_____ 10. We try new ways of dealing with problems.
_____ 11. We feel very close to each other.
_____ 12. We jointly make the decisions in our marriage.
_____ 13. We share hobbies and interests together.
_____ 14. Rules change in our marriage.
_____ 15. We can easily think of things to do together as a couple.
_____ 16. We shift household responsibilities from person to person.
_____ 17. We consult each other on our decisions.
_____ 18. It is hard to identify who the leader is in our marriage.
_____ 19. Togetherness is a top priority.
_____ 20. It is hard to tell who does which household chores.

PART II

Ideally, How Would You Like Your Marriage to Be

_____ 21. We would ask each other for help.
_____ 22. When problems arise, I wish we would compromise.
_____ 23. We would approve of each other's friends.
_____ 24. We would be flexible in how we handle our differences.
_____ 25. We would like to do things with each other.
_____ 26. Different persons would act as leaders in our marriage.
_____ 27. We would feel closer to each other than to people outside our family.

____ 28. We would change our way of handling tasks.

____ 29. We would like to spend free time with each other.

____ 30. We would try new ways of dealing with problems.

____ 31. We would feel very close to each other.

____ 32. We would jointly make the decisions in our marriage.

____ 33. We would share hobbies and interests together.

____ 34. Rules would change in our marriage.

____ 35. We could easily think of things to do together as a couple.

____ 36. We would shift household responsibilities from person to person.

____ 37. We would consult each other on our decisions.

____ 38. We would know who the leader is in our marriage.

____ 39. Togetherness would be top priority.

____ 40. We could tell who does which household chores.

SCORING

PART I

Your Marriage As It Is Now

1. The odd numbers (1, 3, 5, 7, 9, 11, 13, 15, 17, and 19) relate to the Marital Cohesion (or Togetherness) questions. Add up the points by each to determine your Marital Cohesion Score. Then *circle* it at the *top* of the grid. (For example, if your Marital Cohesion Score was 37, you would mark the grid as shown in the example.)

Marital Cohesion Score (now) _____

2. The even numbers (2, 4, 6, 8, 10, 12, 14, 16, 18, and 20) relate to the Marital Adaptability (or Change) questions. Add up the points by each to determine your Marital Adaptability Score. Then *circle* it on the *left* side of the grid. (For example, if your Marital Adaptability Score was 26, you would mark the grid as shown in the example.)

Marital Adaptability Score (now) _____

3. Now that you have determined and marked the two scores, draw a line from each and see in which square they meet. In our example, the two lines meet in square #6.

PART II

Ideally, How Would You Like Your Marriage to Be

These scores are determined in much the same way. The odd numbers (21, 23, 25, 27, 29, 31, 33, 35, 37, and 39) represent the Ideal Marital Cohesion Score. The even numbers (22, 24, 26, 28, 30, 32, 34, 36, 38, and 40) represent the Ideal Marital Adaptability Score. These scores should be determined and marked with a box. For example, an Ideal Marital Cohesion Score of 43 and an Ideal Marital Adaptability Score of 22 would be marked with boxes around them as shown in the example. A line from each should also be drawn to see in which box these two scores meet. In our example, the two lines meet in square #11.

Ideal Marital Cohesion Score _____
Ideal Marital Adaptability Score _____

EXAMPLE

COHESION

MY MARRIAGE

COHESION

Evaluation

a. Any of the sixteen marriage types are acceptable if both husband and wife desire the same particular type. However, of the sixteen marriage types, the squares in the middle (squares #6, 7, 10, and 11) have been found to be the most *balanced marriages*.

b. The squares indicating *midrange marriages* are the ones on the outer areas of the grid (squares #2, 3, 8, 12, 14, 15, 5, and 9).

c. The squares representing *extreme marriages* are those in the corners (squares #1, 4, 13, and 16) representing the extremes of Cohesion (Togetherness) and Adaptability (Change).

Both husband and wife should fill out the MACES III and compare results. Is the marriage being perceived in the same way? Do the two ideal marriages differ? If so, what constructive changes might be made in the future?

©D. H. Olson, 1985.

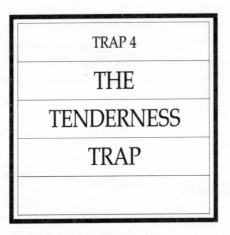

| TRAP 4 |
| THE |
| TENDERNESS |
| TRAP |
| |

Tenderness: The quality of being easily moved to sympathy or compassion; kindness; affection or love.

THE TENDERNESS TRAP: *The inability or unwillingness of a married couple to be kind, loving, caring, or tender with each other.*

A few years ago I was conducting a marriage seminar for a group of married couples. We were discussing love, and I made the observation that it was difficult for many men to tell their wives that they love them. I then asked those attending the seminar if it were true, and if so, why.

Almost everyone agreed that men do not express their love enough to their wives. As to why, some suggested it was unmasculine—not manly. One wife suggested that "men are just not that way." Still another man joked that he didn't have to say it—his wife already knew.

But then there was a pause and a moment of silence, after which one young husband commented, "The reason I don't tell my wife very often that I love her is because she will then know I have feelings!" I thought to myself, "And how tragic it would be if indeed you had feelings but never let her know how you felt."

Many husbands, I believe, are caught in the tenderness trap because they have mistakenly come to believe that being tender is not manly. To be a contemporary male, according to Madison Avenue, a man must either ride horses in a snowstorm and smoke a certain type of cigarette, spend every possible weekend in the mountains drinking beer with his buddies on a campout, or knock down opponents in competitive sports—all to prove that he is a man.

Whenever I have a chance to speak to men about marriage I write the following on the chalkboard: TLC rather than RT. They then ask me what it means, and I translate: Tender Love and Care rather than Rough Treatment.

A great many American males, when they were in high school, had the mistaken notion that young women respond to toughness, abrasiveness, and even cruelty. They thought that supposedly "every girl wants a caveman" and assumed that the worse a boy treated a girl, the more she would like him. Then, after they married, some of them took that philosophy into the relationship.

Many men do not realize today that women deem tenderness, love, and caring as a strength, not a weakness. In essence, it is masculine to be tender, and there are few things more effective that a husband can do to draw his wife near to him than kindness and care for her and their children. Latter-day Saint husbands should be particularly aware of this expectation because the Doctrine and Covenants indicates: "No power or influence can or ought to be maintained by virtue of the priesthood, only by persuasion, by long-suffering, by gentleness and meekness, and by love unfeigned; by kindness, and pure knowledge, which shall greatly enlarge the soul without hypocrisy, and without guile." (D&C 121:41-42.)

It's Tough to Be Tender

A friend of mine once asked me to come and speak to a group of LDS men on marriage. I asked him what topic he wanted me to speak on. He said to choose the most fitting topic I could think of to help a group of LDS husbands in their marriages.

When the time arrived to address the group of men, I was introduced by my friend, who indicated that he did not know the topic on which I would speak. I stood up, greeted the group, and stated the title of my talk: "It's Tough to Be Tender."

I had given a lot of thought to my charge to speak on a topic of major importance to a group of LDS husbands. I began my speech by quoting John 13:34-35, which states that, as disciples of Jesus Christ, we are to become known as a loving people. I then read Paul's commentary of love in 1 Corinthians 13, also found in Moroni 7:44-48, and noted that love means we should be patient, kind, unselfish, and not easily provoked.

After my speech, one of the men in the group stated that such a loving person sounded pretty passive. Another man suggested that such a person may be perceived as a weakling. Others agreed. But I was ready and even anticipated the responses. I had had similar feelings myself at one time.

Men who take upon themselves the discipleship of Christ are going to struggle with some issues of masculinity in our

71

contemporary society. One of my friends, Ida Smith, addressed this topic at a conference held at BYU. Her remarks were later published in the August 1980 issue of the *Ensign*. The article was titled "The Lord As a Role Model for Men and Women." I would recommend that every Latter-day Saint husband and wife read the article, particularly those who struggle with the tenderness/masculinity concept.

In the article she notes:

> We should be careful about assigning mutually exclusive traits to one sex or the other. Nowhere, for example, does the Lord say that tenderness, kindness, charity, faithfulness, patience, gentleness, and compassion are strictly female traits and should be utilized by women only. And nowhere does he say that courage, strength, determination, and leadership should be the exclusive prerogative of men. . . . Since men are also charged to become Christlike, a heavy burden is placed on a man when he realizes that many of the traits that will make him Christlike have been labeled by the world as feminine—and that by taking upon himself those characteristics he runs the risk of having his masculinity seriously questioned by his peers. (Smith, Ida, p. 67.)

Who Cares?

George Bach and Laura Torbet wrote a book titled *A Time for Caring*, in which they note: "In pursuit of the life well-lived many people have ridden roughshod over their own better nature. They have all but trampled their need to care and be cared for. Yet caring for each other—and for ourselves—is essential to the good life. It's an integral part of what we need [in order] to feel at peace with ourselves and the world we live in. By neglecting and trivializing our caring nature, we are betraying our own best interests." (Bach, p. 4.)

The two authors claim we are becoming a noncaring society, a society in which caring for or being tender to others is becoming less important. It is unfashionable and doesn't win popularity contests. Today we lead busy, demanding, and competitive lives. The dog-eat-dog skills that are supposedly

essential for survival in today's society, however, tend to iso-
late people and tend to pit people against each other rather
than bring them closer together.

In *A Time for Caring,* George Bach and Laura Torbet note
that we live inconsistent lives. While many of us can be tender
and caring in our homes and families, we cannot or will not
demonstrate these qualities to the outside world. The opposite also occurs. Furthermore, many have learned to be
superficially caring in the outside world because others will
respond, often in a financial way, to our supposed caring.
Then, when we return home, we fail to demonstrate what
caring skills we do have to those we live with and are around
the most—our spouses and our children. (Bach, p. 4.)

We in the marriage and family field have noted a recent
trend. If you ask the question, "What qualities are essential
for a good marriage?" most people would say such things as
communication, decision making, and conflict resolution.
But we now realize that people can have these skills and yet
use them egotistically for their own self-interest. We have
found too that unless husbands and wives are basically caring
people, all these tools, or skills if you will, are useless.

Alice Robertson has written a paraphrase of 1 Corinthians
13 that illustrates the need for caring:

> Though I may talk glibly about marriage, and have not
> caring, my marriage is still empty.
> I may be able to look into the future and understand the
> dynamics of relationships; I may trust that my marriage will
> not collapse and plan for many new things, but if I have no
> caring, my marriage is nothing.
> I may be unselfish and submit to many changes, yet if I
> have no caring, my marriage is nothing.
> When I care, I am patient and kind, and I am glad for
> the ways in which we differ from each other. When I care, I
> do not always think I am right, and I am willing to defer to
> my spouse graciously.
> When I care, I am slow to react inappropriately, and I
> do not rejoice in getting away with something.
> Caring means commitment in difficult times as well as

73

good times; always looking for the best, expecting the best, and rejoicing in the best.

Thanks be to God that he has made it possible for me to care. (Robertson, p. 5.)

Profiles of a Loving Husband and a Loving Wife

A few years ago I became interested in how married couples convey love and caring for each other. In my *Deseret News* column I invited women readers to write in and tell me what their husbands had done or could do to express love. Nearly one hundred letters came in, and in these letters several types of expressions kept appearing. The students in my classes also made similar responses. From these I compiled a questionnaire and again asked readers to respond to it, ranking the ten most important items of the twenty choices. The results of that questionnaire were published as "Profile of a Loving Husband." (Barlow, *What Wives*, pp. 146-48.) Here are the ten top items, ranked in order of the respondents' choices:

1. He communicates effectively with me by both talking and listening.

2. He expresses his love both by word and action.

3. He expresses affection by touch without sexual overtones.

4. He takes an active part in rearing and disciplining our children.

5. He helps me attain my spiritual needs.

6. He is concerned about my changing intellectual, emotional, social, and physical needs.

7. He encourages rather than discourages my individual endeavors.

8. He often spends time alone with me without interruptions or distractions.

9. He gives genuine help around the house without being asked and without complaining.

10. He helps me attain sexual satisfaction in our relationship.

While surveying wives, I also asked the same questions of husbands: What had their wives done or what could they do to express their love and care? From these I compiled the ten most important items in the order indicated by husbands who responded to the survey. This list was published as "Profile of a Loving Wife." (Barlow, *What Husbands*, pp. 131-33.)

1. She expresses her love both by word and action.
2. She helps me attain my spiritual needs.
3. She supports me in my endeavors both at home and at work.
4. She gives our children adequate emotional and physical care.
5. She helps me attain sexual satisfaction in our relationship.
6. She communicates effectively both by listening and speaking.
7. She keeps our home reasonably clean and free from excessive clutter.
8. She is patient with me and does not nag or complain excessively.
9. She has high self-esteem.
10. She is aware that her appearance and physical fitness affect how I feel toward her.

Some readers will recognize that, from the responses to my questions and from the two profiles, I eventually wrote the books, *What Wives Expect of Husbands* and *What Husbands Expect of Wives*, published by Deseret Book in 1982 and 1983 respectively.

How to Be a Loving Person

A few years ago at Brigham Young University, the Department of Child Development and Family Relations (CDFR) changed its name to the Department of Family Sciences. Among other things, we in the department wanted to communicate to our associates that the study of marriage and family had attained the level of being a science. Some did and may still question whether the study of human relationships will ever be an exact science since people are not as predictable as chemicals or gases. Still, it is interesting that we have moved beyond admonitions and platitudes in helping people attain more loving relationships.

Such an example may be the science of loving. In 1972 C. H. Swenson explained that there are at least seven ways a person may become more loving, caring, and tender. (Swenson, pp. 86-101.) Note that his list is similar to the "Profile of a Loving Husband" and "Profile of a Loving Wife."

1. Verbal expression of love
2. Self-disclosure: reveal personal matters, concerns, and interests
3. Emotional and moral support; interest (nonmaterial)
4. Gifts (material)
5. Physical expression of love: touching, hugging, kissing
6. Tolerance/patience
7. Acts or deeds of kindness

So often people who do not perceive themselves to be loving people often focus on what they are not doing well. If a person wants to be more loving, he or she needs to review C. H. Swenson's list and start practicing some of the things he has suggested. In my estimation, a good place to start would be with number 7, deeds of kindness.

How to Get Out of the Tenderness Trap

If either of you, husband or wife, have a difficult time being kind and caring, you are snared in the tenderness trap. Maybe you are kind and caring to other people, such as your children, neighbors, other family members, or Church members, but not to each other. This may be by choice or by chance, but whatever the reason for your uncaring behavior, remember that you are not only missing out on the best of love and marriage, but you are sowing the seeds for marital destruction.

You can get out of the tenderness trap by starting to do small caring things on a daily basis. The change should be gradual but persistent, and you must believe that change, in time, can occur.

One of the interesting insights on conveying love is in the Bible. It states "let us not love in word, neither in tongue; but in deed."(1 John 3:18.) This admonition, hundreds of years old, is one of the best ways for husbands and wives to convey love—by action or deeds. The following exercise, "Showing Love by Deeds," is based on this biblical principle. The exercise has been adapted from "Caring Days," a chapter in *Helping Couples Change*, by Richard B. Stuart. (Stuart, pp. 192-208.)

A married couple is to sit down and make a list of "loving deeds" or behaviors they would like the other to do or both be willing to do. The deeds they choose are to be (1) specific and understandable, (2) measurable, (3) future oriented (what you want to be), and (4) small enough to be accomplished without exhaustive effort.

The list should contain at least twelve different items, enough items to require a couple to stretch a bit and become more creative. Following is an example of a "Showing Love by Deeds" list put together by a hypothetical couple, Jim and Debbie Allen. They have both contributed to the list and have agreed to complete as many of the items as possible during the next two weeks.

As one person completes one of the items on the "Showing Love by Deeds" list, the other should initial and date the chart. This is to acknowledge the efforts as they are made and also to help each other become more alert to caring efforts.

SHOWING LOVE BY DEEDS
(1 John 3:18)
Names: Jim and Debbie Allen

Desired Deeds	Acknowledged by Debbie	Acknowledged by Jim
1. Ask how I spent the day		
2. Buy me an inexpensive gift (less than $5.00)		
3. Say please and thank you during the day		

 4. Hug, touch, or kiss me daily   _____ _____

 5. Take a half-hour walk with me   _____ _____

 6. Sit by me in church (no chil-
    dren between us)   _____ _____

 7. Call me during the day   _____ _____

 8. Have a twenty-minute conver-
    sation with me each day   _____ _____

 9. Go with me to a movie of my
    choice   _____ _____

10. Get up with the baby every
    other time when he cries at
    night   _____ _____

11. Give me a back rub   _____ _____

12. Help arrange for me to have
    two hours alone   _____ _____

After two weeks, review the "Showing Love by Deeds" exercise. How many loving behaviors were you each able to accomplish? Which ones would you like to continue during the next two weeks? What new ones would you like to add? Remember the requirements. They must be (1) specific and understandable, (2) measurable, (3) future oriented (what you want to be), and (4) small enough to be accomplished without exhaustive effort.

Congratulations on your efforts to become more loving and tender people!

TRAP 5

THE

TALK

TRAP

Talk: To communicate or exchange ideas or information by speaking; to consult or confer.

THE TALK TRAP: *The inability or unwillingness to do much more than exchange information with a marriage partner on a routine, day-to-day basis.*

T he story is told of two hardened prisoners who were locked in a small cell together in Alcatraz Prison for several years. During their imprisonment they got along fairly well, talked frequently, had relatively few conflicts, and endured the prison terms together. When one prisoner was about to be released, he was interviewed by the prison warden. Much to the surprise of the officer, the prisoner being released knew little, in fact practically nothing, about his fellow cell mate. They had lived together in a small cell of just a few cubic feet for years and had exchanged enough information with each other to exist and get by. Even though they had spent tens of thousands of hours together in each other's presence, they scarcely knew anything about each other's personal lives, their backgrounds, or their feelings.

The story points out the fallacy of believing that just because two people live with and are around each other for hours and hours, they will get to know each other. Often they don't because they are prisoners of a different sort, prisoners who are confined each day to their own thoughts, feelings, and ideas.

Contrast these "prisoners" with people who, for instance, meet on an airplane, and within the space of a few hours have conveyed more to each other, about each other, than they have with many other acquaintances, including spouses. Conclusion? The actual amount of time a couple spends together is no measurement of their ability to communicate with each other.

An Irish Divorce

The inability or unwillingness of a married couple to share their lives and their feelings might have another name. It could be called an "Irish divorce."

One summer I was in Ireland representing Brigham Young University and giving a few speeches on marriage and family. I spoke in both the north and south of the Emerald Isle.

While I was in the Irish Republic, I had the opportunity of traveling around with President Vernon Tipton and his wife, Norma, who were presiding over the Ireland Dublin Mission. One afternoon I also met John Connolly, president of the Irish District, who lived in Dublin.

During our conversation I asked President Connolly what the divorce rate was in the south of Ireland. Imagine my astonishment when he replied, "Zero."

"You mean to say that there are no divorces in the Irish Republic?" I asked in amazement.

"That's correct."

I thought for a few moments. I was aware of the strong family solidarity in Ireland because I had observed it when I served an LDS mission there several years ago. But no divorces?

"Do you want to know why there are no divorces in Ireland?" President Connolly asked.

"I have been wondering."

"It's illegal . . . against the law. There are no provisions in the law for divorce in the Irish Republic."

I had heard that divorce was still illegal in some European countries but had no idea that such was the case in Ireland.

After a few more moments of thought I asked, "But what do you do in this country when a husband and wife can't get along? When they won't talk to each other or when they fight and argue a lot?"

President Connolly again replied, "Those situations do occur on occasion. Not often, but on occasion. And then we have what we call an Irish divorce. That's when a man and woman can't get along in marriage but they continue to live together . . . miserable though married. They don't talk much to each other, and they seldom go anywhere together. Publicly, few may know the condition of the marriage. There is no legal separation, but psychologically and emotionally they leave each other. That is what we call an Irish divorce."

The week I was in Ireland divorce legislation was introduced in the government of the Irish Republic. It will likely be a matter of time before divorces are legal there. In the meantime, those who can afford to travel to England, Scotland, or some other country can get a divorce if they want one. And if they want to remarry, they have to go to another country for that as well. But the few who desire to end their marriages do not travel elsewhere to legally separate. They just remain at home and live with the "Irish divorce"—married, but miserable; together, but separated; talking to each other, but not communicating.

As I flew over the Atlantic Ocean a few days later, I thought about my conversation with President Connolly concerning the "Irish divorce," and I came to the conclusion that we also have "Irish divorces" in the United States.

Differences in Communication

One root of communication problems in marriage may be that husbands and wives might perceive the function of communication differently. Casey Peterson, editor of *Marriage Encounter Magazine*, has recently made these observations:

> Mark Sherman and Adelaide Haas are both associate professors at the State University of New York in New Paltz (psychology and communication respectively). [They] recently did a study of communication between the sexes which sheds some light on our differences. Their research ["Man to Man, Woman to Woman," *Psychology Today*, June 1984] concludes that "these (communication) problems are particularly resistant to solution. Not only do men and women like to talk about different topics, spoken language serves different functions for the sexes."
>
> The least important problem in the study was that of topics of interest. Most men surveyed preferred to discuss music, current events and sports. Most women generally talked about relationship problems, family health, reproductive concerns, weight, food and clothing. Both sexes were interested in talking about work, movies and television.
>
> *Isn't it interesting that, in general, men prefer to talk about things outside of themselves, whereas most women would rather*

discuss topics of a personal nature? When I think about that, I see it's very easy for me to advise Tom Landry on offensive strategy on a Sunday afternoon. What am I risking? It's also very easy to discuss the merits of a Carter versus a Weber carburetor, but the thought of telling someone how I feel makes me feel uncomfortable. Why do you suppose that is?

The more serious potential problem in intimate male-female relationships is the difference in the function of conversation between the sexes. According to the survey what men enjoy most in conversation with friends is freedom, playfulness, camaraderie and practicality. While many women mentioned these items, what they valued most was empathy or understanding in their conversations. Furthermore, women not only liked, but truly needed this. . . .

I think [my wife and I] had a rather typical background. We had had most of our conversations with friends of the same sex. I was used to fast-paced conversations that were practical, pragmatic or fun, and usually stayed on the surface with respect to emotions. Debbie [my wife] had practical and fun conversations too, but they were also a major source of emotional support and understanding. So I tended to be direct and practical and Debbie wanted a sympathetic listener. I wanted to fix all her problems and often said, "Here's what ya do." The same thing I'd say to all my friends. In short, I was an advice-giver, not a listener.

We struggled along like that for several years until I learned to ask for what I needed, and to really listen to what Debbie was saying. *Most of the time what Debbie wants and needs is emotional support and understanding, not advice.* . . . Once in a while she does ask me for some advice and that makes me feel good that she values my opinion. . . . What we've both learned is to state our needs—if I want support I ask for it. If I want advice I ask for that. (Peterson, Casey, pp. 4-5. Italics added.)

One of the first steps we must take in communicating effectively is to realize that husbands and wives may talk and listen for different reasons. Certainly not all communication is for the exchange of information only.

Differences in communication also occur because talking usually takes place on one of four levels: (1) things, (2) people,

(3) ideas, and (4) feelings. Most of our conversations deal with levels one and two: things and people. These are the safest and take the least amount of involvement. We talk about the weather, the ball game, our yard and garden, our neighbors and friends, our children and relatives because we usually have something to say about them. But moving to levels three and four—ideas and feelings—is much more difficult. Nevertheless, discussion in these two areas is what typically forms the strongest bonds. Discussion about things and people usually does not.

Discussing ideas and feelings may sometimes be difficult to do. It would be fairly safe to say that most readers of this book are honest people, yet in many ways the same people are dishonest when it comes to being open about feelings and ideas. Most people who would not cheat, steal, or knowingly tell lies would not hesitate to answer "Fine!" when their spouses ask them how they are. Burdening other people with our burdens, complaining, disagreeing in public—these are things we think should be avoided, but we may be carrying the principle of avoidance too far.

If we are burdened by financial problems, keeping them from our spouses may only increase the weight of the burden and prevent necessary support. Reporting praise we've received at work but neglecting to talk about some problems we've been having with the boss may increase our stress and deceive our spouse into thinking everything's perfect at work. Most of us can probably attain a better balance between honesty and tactfulness about our feelings and ideas. That is, we can still avoid overcomplaining and burdening people with petty details but be more open about the things that really matter.

Two Important Communication Skills

Whenever I discuss communication with married people in classes or seminars, I like to first ask them what they think are important communication skills. The responses usually range from "Use *I* messages and speak for self," or "Be aware of your nonverbal communication or body language." These are important in effective communication, but I think they are secondary to two other very important communication skills. One is caring, and the other is listening.

Caring. Think for a moment about people who care about you. With them you are much more likely to open up, to relate your innermost thoughts and feelings. Think about one of your best friends, a family member, or perhaps a concerned teacher or coach. Are you not much more likely to be willing to talk to these trusted individuals than to the numerous people you interact with daily who show little or no personal interest in you?

Think for a moment too about people you really care about. With them aren't you more likely to take the time and effort to communicate accurately and avoid misunderstandings? Don't you find yourself interested in their lives and what they have to say? Even with young children who don't yet know how to talk well, most parents listen carefully far more often than they refuse to listen.

If caring is the key to effective communication, and I suggest it is, then we would improve our communication skills by becoming more caring people. It is no accident that the chapter on tenderness and caring precedes this one on communication.

Listening. Another way to dramatically improve communication in marriage is to improve our listening skills. Many of us believe we are good listeners just because we keep quiet when someone is speaking. Even so, our attention may be elsewhere or may be divided between what is being said and what happened a few hours earlier. Or perhaps the television is on, or the newspaper is spread out. In those cases, is our attention undivided? The Japanese have an interesting custom when they talk. The one listening will intermittently interrupt with the words *hai* or *eh*. The interruptions let the speaker know the other person is listening. When we listen we might try rephrasing what is said to let the speaker know where our concentration is.

Married couples may also get into a peculiar habit of conversing about two different things at the same time. The wife may talk about a luncheon date, while the husband may talk about the upcoming football race. Each is more intent on what he or she is saying than on what the spouse is saying. The spouses may even end the conversation without knowing what their partners have discussed. Paying attention to our spouses when they are talking is not only a courtesy but is also an important key to sharing and understanding.

Hearing or Listening?

Anyone wishing to improve his or her communication skills may want to read Mortimer Adler's book *How to Speak; How to Listen.* He has some very practical suggestions, particularly on listening. He notes that of the four major communication skills—reading, writing, speaking, and listening—we spend approximately nine percent of our time writing, fifteen percent reading, thirty percent speaking, and forty-six percent listening. Even though we spend nearly half of our communicative efforts in listening, it is the area in which we have the least training. Adler notes: "If asked why this is so, one response may be that instruction in writing played a part in his schooling and that some attention, though much less (to a degree that is both striking and shocking) was paid to developing the skills of reading and speaking. Almost no attention at all was given to skill in listening. Another response may be forthcoming from the person who reveals the mistaken impression that listening involves little more than keeping quiet while the other person talks. Good manners may be required, but not much skill." (Adler, pp. 88-89.)

Adler offers these insights and notes the importance of concentration in effective listening:

> The ears have nothing comparable to eyelids, but they can be as effectively sealed as eyelids can be closed. Sometimes both close at the same time, but it is often the case that the ear is turned off while the eyes are open. That matters

little if, in either case, the mind's attention is turned to other matters than what is being heard or seen. What the senses register are then sounds and sights that lack significance.

Listening, like reading, is primarily an activity of the mind, not of the ear or the eye. When the mind is not actively involved in the process, it should be called hearing, not listening; seeing, not reading. (Adler, pp. 85-86.)

Dr. Adler suggests that a major mistake most people make in listening is in regarding it as passive reception rather than as active participation. He then gives a vivid analogy of his observation:

The catcher behind the plate is just as active a baseball player as the pitcher on the mound. The same is true in football of the end who receives the forward pass and the back who throws it. Receiving the ball in both cases requires actively reaching to complete the play. Catching is as much an activity as throwing and requires as much skill, though it is a skill of a different kind. Without the complementary efforts of both players, properly attuned to each other, the play cannot be completed. . . .

Of course, the fault may not always lie with the reader or listener. The failure to catch a wild pitch is not the catcher's fault. So, too, some pieces of writing and some spoken utterances are either so devoid of meaning and coherence or so befuddled and confusing in their use of words that the best reader and listener can make little sense of them. Some are such defective presentations of what is in the mind of the speaker that they are not worth paying much attention to, if any at all. (Adler, pp. 86-87.)

To assist two people to become better speakers and listeners, Mortimer Adler has devised what he calls the "Meeting of the Minds." The first rule he gives is "Do not disagree—or, for that matter, do not agree—with anyone else unless you are sure you understand the position the other person is taking. To disagree before you understand is impertinent. To agree is inane." (Adler, p. 159.) Here is the "Meeting of the Minds" exercise:

| PARTNER A | PARTNER B |

PARTNER A

1. Takes a stand or gives an opinion on a particular topic or issue.

2. States two or three reasons for the particular position.

PARTNER B

1. Listens attentively and responds appropriately:
   a. Restates Partner A's position.
   b. Restates reasons for Partner A's position.

2. Reacts by either agreeing or disagreeing.

 3. If disagrees, states two or three reasons for the disagreement.

1. Listens attentively and responds appropriately:
   a. Restates Partner B's position.
   b. Restates reasons for Partner B's position.

2. Reacts by either agreeing or disagreeing.

3. If disagrees, states two or three reasons for the dis- agreement.

This process continues until Partner A and Partner B clarify the areas of agreement and disagreement.

Couples may want to practice this exercise by having one person, Partner A, state an opinion on a particular matter and then give reasons for the particular point of view. The second person, Partner B, would then repeat not only Partner A's opinion but also the stated reasons. When this has been done to Partner A's satisfaction, Partner B may then either agree or disagree. If he or she agrees, a meeting of the minds has occurred. If he or she disagrees, Partner B would state the differing opinion and give the reasons for so believing. Then Partner A would repeat Partner B's position and the stated reasons. This process continues until both partners know the exact position of the other on a given issue and can give the other's reasons for belief. At this point, too, a meeting of the minds has occurred.

How to Get Out of the Talk Trap

As a married couple you are in the talk trap if you seldom take the opportunity to discuss anything other than the routine and mechanics of day-to-day living (levels 1–things and 2–people). To get out of the trap, start sharing a little more of your thoughts on the third and fourth levels, ideas and feelings.

Following is an exercise to help you do this. Many couples have tried it and reported excellent results in having more in-depth conversations with a marriage partner.

COMMUNICATION ON SPIRITUAL MATTERS

Instructions: The incomplete sentences in the list below are designed to help you and your partner talk about your religious feelings, attitudes, and beliefs. Look over the list and decide together which sentence you will discuss. Then take turns completing the sentence. (You may want to do so first by writing rather than by talking.) After you have discussed one sentence, select another and do the same. Do not, however, try to discuss all the topics in one sitting. Save some for another in-depth communication experience.

1. I feel the closest to you spiritually when _____

2. I feel closest to Deity (God, the Father) when _____

3. I feel the most inspired when _____

4. Religion helps me to enjoy life because _____

5. The religious beliefs that mean the most to me are _____

6. Participation in church activities is important to me because
_____

7. In the spiritual area the things I'd like to do more with you are
_____

8. The ways you could help me attain my spiritual needs are
_____

9. The most spiritual experiences I have had thus far in life are
_____

10. The most spiritual experiences we have had together thus far in
our marriage are _____

11. The way I feel about prayer is _____

12. Our prayers have been answered when _____

13. We could increase our spirituality together by _____

14. Participation with other adults in religious activities is important because _____

15. The times I feel most hopeful are _____

16. The things that are most worth living for right now are
_____

17. The most inspirational religious books I have read are _____
_____

18. The ways we could develop spirituality in our children are
_____

19. What I really feel about Deity (God, the Father) is _____

20. Other matters relating to spirituality I'd like to discuss with you
are _____

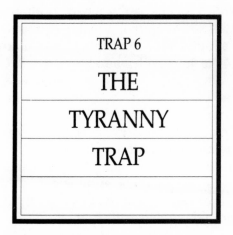

TRAP 6

THE

TYRANNY

TRAP

Tyranny: Arbitrary or unrestrained exercise of power; despotic abuse of authority.

THE TYRANNY TRAP: *The tendency of one marriage partner to exercise too much power or control in decision making.*

O ne interesting aspect of marriage in America is how married couples go about making decisions. Several years ago, Robert O. Blood completed a study of decision making and found that about sixty percent of the marriages were "equalitarian"—where both husband and wife participated in the decision-making process. As might be expected, about twenty percent of the marriages were "patriarchal"—the husband made all of the decisions. The unexpected finding of his study, however, was that about twenty percent of the marriages were "matriarchal"—the wife made all of the decisions. Mr. Blood suggested that the percentage of matriarchal marriages in the United States was unusual and would not be found in such large numbers in any other country. Whether the trends or percentages have changed significantly since his study is not known. What is known is that there are a variety of ways that husbands and wives go about making decisions in their marriages.

Husbands As Head of the House

The next time you are at some kind of gathering with other married couples and the conversation starts to get dull, bring up a question that should stir some discussion: "Should the man be the head of the house?" Tradition would say "yes," and many couples, I find, are still quite traditional. I ask this question in my marriage seminars, and the majority of both husbands and wives, about sixty to seventy percent, say "yes." But the hesitancy of the responses is what interests me, particularly among the women. Some will say "yes, sort of," or "in most circumstances," or "most of the time."

Then comes the next question: "In what way should the man be the head of the house?" During a marriage seminar in Sacramento, California, we had a lively discussion of this topic and came up with the following ways a husband could be the "head of the house":

The King. This model is the "so let it be written, so let it be done" type—sort of the Yul Brynner model in the movie *The King and I.* The husband's word is law, and there is no disputation, no argument from either wife or children. If or when there is a question of authority, the consequences might be the "off-with-their-heads" philosophy. Good kings might be tolerated by their supposed subjects; bad kings are despised.

Benevolent Dictator. This type of leader is one notch below the King. He is a nice guy, however, and fairly easygoing as long as things go his way. He still wants to be in control and resorts to less noticeable and punitive tactics than the King to get it. Both types rule with "unrighteous dominion" (see D&C 121:39); they just go about it differently.

Impasse Arbitrator. The man who leads in this manner is kind, relaxed, and doesn't get much involved with either marriage or family affairs until an impasse is encountered and a decision needs to be made. Then he puts on his arbitration cloak and mentality and tries to negotiate a solution. He is of the "Bo-Peep" persuasion that, with marriage and family problems, "you leave them alone until they come home." Then he becomes involved as a Johnny-come-lately leader.

Mayor/Political Boss. Most everyone knows that in national, state, and local government there is a designated leader. He or she usually becomes such by popular vote, which is a form of social sanction. They appear to be leading and in charge. But almost everyone knows that in many forms of government there is also a political boss—someone who is not designated or elected, but who essentially runs the show. In many marriages, the husband is the mayor, designated as such socially, religiously, and economically. But most family members, including himself, realize that his wife—the mother—is the political boss and wields the true power in family decision making.

Chairman of the Board. This individual presides over the group but is little more than a manager who carries out the wishes of the board (sometimes also spelled b-o-r-e-d). His vote or input is often minimal, but still he is officially designated as the "chair." In marriage, some husbands operate similarly in that the family decides what they want and assigns Dad to carry out the assignment. But a chairman of the board is usually easy to get along with as long as he receives public recognition through periodic gifts such as gold watches and public announcements that he is still the chairman of the board.

Limited Partnership. In this marriage, the husband says he believes in equality between himself and his wife. The reality is, however, that he still wants to be "a little more equal" than his wife by maintaining a 51/49 percent split in the stock. Even though they outwardly appear, and nearly are, equal, he is still in charge with the additional two percent of the stock that gives him the majority, and also the control, of the partnership.

Guide/Scout. The guide/scout type of leader is one who leads the group but is often absent while performing his duties. He frequently points out the direction, and then "Hi-Ho, Silver," he is away. Another way to detect the guide/scout type of leader is to watch for the man who always walks in front of his wife and children. Sometimes he will even walk into church and sit down without them. A few minutes later, his wife and children open the chapel doors and follow in his footsteps to their seats. A guide/scout truly leads, but he is seldom with the wagon train.

While the previous seven types of leaders have been described tongue-in-cheek, there are two other ways a man can lead. These two have significance for Latter-day Saints and other Christians as well.

The Bishop. One time I attended a conference on family life in Milwaukee, Wisconsin, and was intrigued by a Catholic priest who related his understanding that, in the early Christian church, religious communities were made up of Christian homes with an "episcopate" or bishop (father of the home) in charge. I had made a similar analogy a few years ago in my article "Strengthening the Patriarchal Order in the Home." (See Barlow, "Strengthening," pp. 29-33.) In it I noted that bishops do not necessarily make all the decisions for those over whom they preside. They listen to their counselors and then see that the decisions are made and based upon righteous principles. Bishops do not always become involved in decisions that could be made by others called to serve. Moses was taught this manner of leading by his father-in-law, Jethro. (See Ex. 18:13-26.)

The Servant of All. As head of the house, there is still one type of leader that ought to be considered by all husbands and particularly those who confess discipleship of Jesus Christ. It is called the Servant of All and is described in Matthew 20:20-28. There it states that the mother of James and John came to Jesus and requested that her two sons be given superior status to the other ten apostles, that one might sit on Jesus' right hand and the other on his left. Jesus told the woman that she did not understand the consequences of such a request, and then he stated that the world operates on the principle of dominion while heaven operates on the principle of service. Those who are supposedly great, he noted, exercise authority and dominion over others, but in his kingdom it was not to be so: "Whosoever will be great among you, let him be your minister; and whosoever will be chief among you, let him be your servant." Such leadership, however, is only for the emotionally mature and deeply committed disciples of Christ. Who would not follow one who serves selflessly for the good of all?

Do Men Have Superior Judgment?

Unfortunately, the belief that men are superior to women goes back several hundred years in history, and many people are unaware of the inferior status women have had and still retain in many countries.

Aristotle wrote in his time, "The male is by nature superior, and the female inferior; and the one rules and the other is ruled. . . . The male is by nature fitter for command than the female. . . . We must look to the female as being a sort of natural deficiency."

Rousseau, the French philosopher, also noted, "Woman is especially constituted to please men. . . . to be useful to them, to make themselves loved and honored by them, to

95

educate them when young, to care for them when grown, to counsel them, to console them and to make life agreeable and sweet to them—these are the duties of women at all times, and what should be taught them from infancy."

Blackstone, the jurist, wrote in his famous *Commentaries* that "the very being or legal existence of woman is incorporated and consolidated into that of the husband; under whose wing, protection and *cover*, she performs everything." Milton, the English poet, observed, "It is no small glory to him [man], that a creature [woman] so like him should be made subject to him."

But it has not only been men who perpetuated the superiority-of-men belief. A nineteenth-century Englishwoman wrote, "The most perfect and implicit faith in the superiority of a husband's judgment, and the most absolute obedience of his desires, is not only the conduct that will ensure the greatest successes, but will give the most entire satisfaction." (Lederer, pp. 61-62.)

In the past, even as late as 1919, the vast majority of men and most of the women believed that men are not only superior to women, but should also direct their affairs and make decisions for them as well. Unfortunately, these ideas still persist in the minds of some men.

In their interesting book, *The Mirages of Marriages*, William J. Lederer and Don D. Jackson observe: "The rigid, male-dictated marital structure of the eleventh and twelfth centuries cannot function in today's environment. Neither can the extreme feminist dream of female domination. Modern marriage requires equality, just as world history indicates a trend toward equality among people regardless of sex, race, or creed." (Lederer, p. 18.)

They conclude, "The question of who has the right to do what to whom—and when—is the pervasive, nagging issue which must be worked out by every couple, for it arises daily. A set of relationship rules must be agreed upon. In the formulation of these rules, each individual must feel that he has a right, equal to the other's right, to determine what goes on. A person who feels that he is being controlled, denied the rights of reasonable self-determination, will fight—overtly or covertly—to regain control. History (of both marriages and nations) repeatedly has shown that systems based on an unequal division of power eventually fall. To survive a system requires mutual responsibility, reward, security, and dignity." (Lederer, p. 17.)

Who Decides?

There once was a question we asked in marriage that is now outdated. We used to say, "Who wears the pants in your family?" which meant who is the boss or who makes the decisions? We cannot, however, continue asking the question for two basic reasons. First, with the fashion changes, women and men both wear pants now, so the question is inappropriate. Second, women are now also making and helping make more of the decisions in marriage.

You will recall from "Trap 2: The Tradition Trap" that two types of marriages were described: the traditional marriage and the companionship marriage. The traditional marriage features a one-vote system in which the husband makes all major decisions. The companionship marriage features a two-vote system in which the husband and wife share decision making. As was noted in that chapter, we are rapidly moving toward the second system in contemporary marriages.

In his book *Helping Couples Change,* Dr. Richard Stuart has made an interesting observation about decision making in marriage. He notes: "The changing situational demands of daily living, the evolution of our bodies and ourselves, and the shifts in cultural patterns and values all call for kaleidoscopic adaptations by partners in successful marriages. It is simply not possible to sustain on their 10th anniversary the same strategies for coping with most areas of their functioning that the couple negotiated during their honeymoon. Therefore, every couple must have in their kit of survival skills the ability to make decisions constructively and efficiently." (Stuart, p. 252.)

Who makes most of the decisions in your marriage? There are literally dozens of situations we face daily that require some kind of decision. How those decisions are made can either enhance or undermine the marital relationship. Dr. Stuart has identified five major categories in decision making:

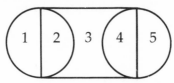

(1) Husband only decides, (2) Husband decides after consulting with wife, (3) Both decide together, (4) Wife decides after consulting with husband, and (5) Wife only decides. (Stuart, p. 267.) The categories 1 and 5 are extremes and represent an imbalance of power in a marriage.

Sometimes a couple will need to discuss which category their decision making falls into. One of my students stopped by my office to talk about a decision her husband had recently made. She was furious—her husband had just graduated from college and was offered a job on the east coast, which he had accepted without even asking her opinion. When she asked him about his isolated decision, he simply replied, "It's my job, isn't it?" He thought that accepting a job was a decision in Category 1, "Husband only decides." His wife, on the other hand, thought it should be a decision in Category 2, "Husband decides after consulting wife," or even in Category 3, "Both decide together," since she had personal reasons for not wanting to go to the eastern part of the United States. Had the husband merely asked his wife her opinion about moving, the situation would have been less tense. She ended up moving with him anyway, but his arrogance in thinking it was his decision only was what concerned his wife the most.

Following is a list of questions a married couple frequently face. (See also Stuart, pp. 266-67.) For insights into your own marriage, go through the list and indicate with a 1, 2, 3, 4, or 5 next to each question how the decision is being made. Use the categories of decision making given previously. After you have completed that part, go over the list of questions again and indicate in the same manner how you would like the decisions to be made.

For example, by question 14 on major financial purchases, if the husband only is making that decision, write down a 1 under the column, "Who currently makes the decision?" The second time through, however, if the person doing the evaluating would like that to be a "Both decide together" decision, write down a 3 under the column, "Who should make the decision?"

1-Husband only decides; 2-Husband decides after consulting with wife; 3-Both decide together; 4-Wife decides after consulting with husband; 5-Wife only decides

Area	Who currently makes the decision?	Who should make the decision?
1. Where couple lives		
2. What job husband takes		
3. How many hours husband works		
4. Whether wife works		
5. What job wife takes		
6. How many hours wife works		
7. How many children in family		
8. When to have children		
9. How and when to discipline children		
10. How much time to spend with children		
11. How much time to spend with family and friends		
12. When to have sexual relationships		
13. How to spend money		
14. When to make major financial purchases		
15. How much money to donate to church or charity		
16. How much time to spend in church activities		

17. How much time to spend in
    community activities   _____ _____
18. How much time to spend in
    personal pursuits   _____ _____
19. Where and when to go on
    vacations   _____ _____
20. Other: _____ _____ _____
21. Other: _____ _____ _____
22. Other: _____ _____ _____

When both husband and wife complete this exercise and then compare notes, they can quickly see how the decision making operates in their marriage and also recommend what changes might be made. Both may want more involvement in some decisions and less in others.

Obviously marriage partners will not always agree on who should make what decisions. But more importantly, can you both now agree on how you could change the decision-making process in your marriage should you need to make some adjustments? Until a husband and wife know each other's expectations in many aspects of marriage, including decision making, attaining marital satisfaction is difficult. Is there currently an imbalance in decision making in your marriage? Were most of your answers either Category 1, "Husband only decides," or Category 5, "Wife only decides"? If so, you may be caught in the tyranny trap. Contemporary marriage will likely be more satisfying for both husband and wife if there is a balance in the decision-making process.

Many married couples believe that the ideal marriage would operate most out of Category 3, "Both decide together." This philosophy is questionable. We should be careful not to overload our marriage with the trivia of the day. There are many decisions in almost all marriages that could and should be categories 1, 2, 4, and 5. That would leave Category 3 for a few of the most essential areas, ones that require considerable deliberation or discussion.

In our own marriage, we have found that many decisions are best made by one person. For example, Susan makes

100

most, if not all, of the decisions about food purchases. She is good at it, understands nutrition, and is a shrewd shopper. We lose money and do not eat well when I shop for food.

My wife, on the other hand, has agreed that I make the decisions about our automobiles. She has one major goal in mind when she gets in the car. She wants to turn on the key and go. If the car has oil in it, fine. If not, no big deal. She can ignore the blinking red light on the dashboard since I have agreed to assume the responsibility for keeping oil in the cars.

In most marriages there are many areas in which one partner has greater talents, skills, or interests than the other. These should be put to use if both can agree who should be deciding what. Remember, the one who assumes the responsibility for making a 1, 2, 4, or 5 decision usually has the responsibility for implementing the decision once it is made. When this dimension is considered, people are less prone to assume too much responsibility for decision making in the marriage.

What, then, are the areas of major importance that require both husband and wife to participate in the decision-making process (Category 3)? Deciding how to discipline children is usually one area in which both should participate. Another would be major purchases involving large sums of money. It is a rare marriage today that has either husband or wife in total control of family finances. Other areas might include family moves, areas relating to employment, education for children or spouses. Another sensitive area that should be in Category 3, "Both decide together," is #12, "When to have sexual relationships."

During the past few years that I have been writing my newspaper column, I have received many letters from readers. Many wish to comment, question, or elaborate on something I have written. The letters have been very helpful in keeping me informed with what is going on in marriages today.

On occasion, however, I receive letters that cause me a great deal of concern. Such was the occasion not long ago when I received a letter regarding something I had written about the importance of touch in relationships. I commented that most human beings have a need both to touch and to be touched. I also made the observation that while touching, hugging, and caressing are common before marriage, many contemporary married people become nearly nontactual after marriage. The only time some married couples touch, I observed, is for routine, somewhat mechanical sexual relationships. The letter I received concerning this is as follows:

> Dear Dr. Barlow:
>
> A few weeks ago you wrote about touch in relationships, and I want to share my experience (anonymously) with you and your readers. We have been married thirteen years and have seven children. My husband recently decided that passion has no place in marriage. He will only allow sexual intimacy twice a month but no form of touch, petting, or passion before. He has decided that nudity during lovemaking in marriage is inappropriate. He believes all this is a "higher law."
>
> I feel he is misguided, and I am really dissatisfied. Isn't touch and nudity appropriate and even necessary in contemporary marriage? Thank you.

This marriage, I thought after reading the letter, is in trouble. The couple may not necessarily divorce, but it is evident to me that they will separate emotionally if they have not done so already unless they can resolve the husband's tyranny and the lack of intimacy in the marriage.

The husband in this particular marriage is caught in a trap of his own making. (See "Trap 10: The Touch Trap.") With his rigid and somewhat sexist approach to intimacy in marriage, which he thinks is a higher law, he is destroying the very relationship he so naively believes he is elevating to a higher level.

Since when, in contemporary marriage, does a husband decide he will "allow sexual intimacy twice a month"? That philosophy went out with high-button shoes! I thought the idea that "sex is a man's prerogative and a woman's duty" had ended long ago. Apparently it has not.

As for the nudity in marriage, there is a Biblical verse, Genesis 2:25, that may have some relevance. Of Adam and Eve, the first married couple mentioned in the Bible, it simply states: "And they were both naked, the man and his wife, and were not ashamed." What can I add to that?

Remember, save Category 3, "Both decide together," for the major areas of common interest such as sexual relationships. Relegate as many other decisions as possible to the 1, 2, 4, and 5 categories (be careful of 1 and 5 though!). By so doing, you may be adding some oil to what otherwise might be a rusty marital relationship.

Years ago there was a popular television program titled *Father Knows Best*. Rather ironically, the father in the program was the one who didn't always know best. The belief that father always knows best, just because he is a man or the father, is fast disappearing. Most have realized that wives and mothers know just as much if not more. Contemporary women want their thoughts and opinions given due consideration.

Some Thoughts for Latter-day Saints

As I have discussed Dr. Stuart's categories in decision making with some Latter-day Saint couples, I have been amazed that some husbands perceive the patriarchal marriage as a Category 1, "Husband only decides." We then discuss how good marriages operate out of all five categories. Some husbands sometimes have a difficult time deciding what Category 5 issues are. What are "Wife only decides" areas for Latter-day Saint women? Some of the answers I have heard have often been simplistic and demeaning.

I would suggest that every Latter-day Saint couple read or reread the excellent article by Elder Dean L. Larsen titled "Marriage and the Patriarchal Order" in the *Ensign*, September 1982, pp. 6-13. In it he related the following incident:

Recently I was visited in my office by a young woman at whose forthcoming temple marriage I had been invited to officiate. She was distraught and tearful and disclosed that she had some serious questions about whether she should go ahead with the marriage. As we discussed the reasons for these questions, the young prospective bride told me of a conversation she had had the previous evening with her fiance. In a fashion uncharacteristic of their relationship, he had, at the insistence of his father, he said, laid down the law and the conditions that would have to prevail in their marriage. He was to be the unquestioned authority. His word would be *law*. She was to be willing to submit to his rule. It was important, he said, that she understand these conditions which would now be imposed on her by covenant in the temple ceremony.

It was interesting to me that this young man, who had won the hand and the heart of this sweetheart though a loving and gentle courtship, now was constrained to impose a strict dominion upon her. In so doing he was appealing to his *misunderstanding* of the patriarchal order, for there could hardly have been a greater distortion or misrepresentation of the actual conditions that must prevail within that order. (Larsen, "Marriage," p. 8. Italics added.)

On this particular topic, Doctrine and Covenants 121: 34-38, 41 has something vital to consider:

Behold, there are many called, but few are chosen. And why are they not chosen?

Because their hearts are set so much upon the things of this world, and aspire to the honors of men, that they do not learn this one lesson—that the rights of the priesthood are inseparably connected with the powers of heaven, and that the powers of heaven cannot be controlled nor handled only upon the principles of righteousness.

That they may be conferred upon us, it is true; but when we undertake to cover our sins, or to gratify our pride, our vain ambition, or to exercise control or dominion or compulsion upon the souls of the children of men, in any degree of unrighteousness, behold, the heavens withdraw themselves; the Spirit of the Lord is grieved; and when it is withdrawn, Amen to the priesthood or the authority of that man. Behold, ere he is aware, he is left unto himself. . . .

No power or influence can or ought to be maintained by virtue of the priesthood, only by persuasion, by long-suffering, by gentleness and meekness, and by love unfeigned.

How to Get Out of the Tyranny Trap

You are in the Tyranny Trap if (1) there is an imbalance in the decision making in your marriage and (2) you are more concerned with "Who decides?" rather than "What is decided?" By reviewing the categories of decision making, you should get a good idea of how you are approaching decisions with your marriage partner. Perhaps some changes need to be made. A marriage partner may want more involvement in some areas of decision making and less in others. Talk it over at a time when neither of you is emotionally charged. Remember, if changes are going to be made, make them gradually, and be willing to change first.

Some married couples may have a difficult time making decisions by becoming preoccupied with who is going to decide. By so doing, they may ignore the much more important issue of what is decided. Lowell and Carol Erdahl have addressed the problem in "Who Decides What?" First they observe that, traditionally, the man has been seen as the "head" of the house and the wife as the "heart." While they see some merit in this perception, they also offer caution.

> In spite of all that can be said for it, we don't like this "head and heart" arrangement. It suggests that the husband has all the brains and the wife all the emotions. . . .
>
> Being male does not ensure the presence of either love or wisdom. . . . Beyond the wisdom of particular decisions, a wife who yields total responsibility for ultimate decision-making abdicates something essential to her full personhood and, at the same time, gives her husband responsibility he should not have to bear alone. (Erdahl, p. 10.)

The Erdahls ask married couples to be more concerned with the general outcome of the decision, rather than be preoccupied with the issue of who makes it. In helping marriage partners decide, they suggest eleven tests for Christian couples to follow:

—The law test: Is it (the contemplated action) in accordance with the Ten Commandments?

—The Golden Rule test: Is it in accordance with the Golden Rule, "Do unto others as you would have others do unto you"?

—The test of Jesus' new commandment: Is it in accord with Jesus' new commandment to "love one another as I have loved you"?

—The test of consequences: Is it hurtful or helpful to myself and others?

—The test of publicity: Is it something I'd be pleased to have everyone know about?

—The test of respected people: Is it something I'd like those whom I respect the most to know about?

—The test of universality: Would the world be better or worse if everyone were to act the way I'm thinking of acting?

—The test of projected retrospect: Will I likely be pleased five/ten years from now to have done what I'm thinking of doing today?

—The test of Jesus' example: Is it something Jesus would do?

—The test of self-love: Does it express love of neighbor as of self? If I do this, will I be caring as much for others as I care for myself?

—The test of conscience: Will I feel regret or gratitude after the deed is done or left undone? (Erdahl, p. 11.)

The next time you and your spouse confront a major decision, why not apply these eleven tests to your options? It may help you in getting out of the tyranny trap and result in excellent decisions.

TRAP 7

THE

TURMOIL

TRAP

Turmoil: A state of extreme confusion, agitation, or commotion; turbulence or disorder.

THE TURMOIL TRAP: *The inability of a married couple to deal constructively with marital conflict.*

I t has been observed that contemporary marriage presents more opportunity for conflict than almost any other interpersonal relationship. Yet many still cling to the concept that marriage should be free of conflict and that only conflict-free marriages can be considered successful. We are gradually coming to understand, however, that most couples experience adjustments and conflicts in marriage. The problems of conflict actually seem to arise more in how couples confront and deal with disagreement: conflict in marriage is common; dealing adequately with the conflict is not.

How Common Is Conflict in Marriage?

Upon arriving at Brigham Young University in 1977, I began teaching classes on marriage. I had taught similar classes at four other universities before going to BYU. During one of my first classes at BYU, I made the observation that most of the students would probably experience some degree of conflict with their marriage partner once they married.

One young returned missionary was very irritated with my comment on conflict and after class even questioned whether I should be teaching at BYU. It was interesting to me that at no time at any of the other four universities where I had taught, had any student, married or single, questioned the likelihood of conflict in marriage. The young man said he had never observed his parents in any kind of conflict. He said his mission president and his wife appeared to have a conflict-free marriage (though what self-respecting mission president and wife will hash over differences in front of the missionaries?). And what was more, the student said he had talked to married neighbors and not one indicated they had ever experienced any conflict in their marriages.

Such was my introduction to BYU. I found that many students were idealistic when it came to marriage and family matters. Should I tell them "what it is really like," or should I relate the ideal? This is a problem not only for marriage counselors and teachers at BYU but all over the nation. How does one deal with "what should be" compared to "what is"?

My own experience has been that when the ideal becomes so far removed from the real, people become discouraged. We must always keep the ideal before us for goals and growth, but we should never put the ideal so far in front of us that we quit trying. I was somewhat relieved later in that same course when a student wrote a paper about idealism vs. realism at BYU. She concluded her paper with the statement, "What we need in LDS marriages is idealism tempered with realism." Perhaps she said it best.

For married couples to believe that their marriages will be free of conflict is, in my opinion, naive. It is also a myth to believe that the presence of conflict indicates a bad marriage. Marriage counselors have noted that many husbands and wives believe so strongly in such traits as politeness, consideration, and benevolence that they attempt to practice them unremittingly. Small failures then become big failures in their eyes. Obviously, spouses also have different interests, different ways of using time, different biological rhythms, and so on—they cannot always have the same desires, needs, or wishes at the same time.

There may be marriages that have little or no conflict, though many marriages that appear to be free of conflict may be far from ideal. A married couple may have little in common, deriving most of their satisfaction in life from sources outside the marriage. They see each other so infrequently that they have little time to talk, let alone fight. Other than their children and a few daily routines, they find they have little to discuss when they do talk. Since they seldom interact, they rarely differ.

In still another type of marriage a husband and wife may have worked out a dominant/submissive relationship, in which one dominates and controls the other. In other words, one is master, the other is slave. Obviously, a slave rarely disagrees with a master, so they experience little conflict until one or the other tires of the relationship and tries to change things.

Some older couples, much to the amazement of many

younger couples and single adults, claim they have never had an argument. And perhaps they have matured to the point where they have worked through most, if not all of the conflicts. During their earlier years of marriage, however, there likely was some conflict that they have now forgotten or downplayed.

There are couples, too, who avoid public displays of conflict. These couples avoid letting their children know of their differences, settling their disputes privately. Children of such marriages grow up believing that their parents never had arguments.

In the book *Sex and the Significant Americans*, John Cuber and Peggy Harroff have identified what they call utilitarian and intrinsic marriages. In utilitarian marriages the couples are uninvolved with each other because they are highly committed to other endeavors. Couples in the intrinsic marriages have each other as their first priority, are highly involved with each other, and are deeply committed to their marriage. In comparing and contrasting the two marriage types, the authors observe: "Men and women in Intrinsic Marriages experience conflict too. Some of these pairs actually have had more conflict than typically occurs for couples in Utilitarian Marriages. Partly it is simple mathematics. There are more numerous points of contact, hence more potential for conflict. Couples in Utilitarian Marriages often avoid conflict simply because so many important matters are considered private and not even exposed to the spouse." (Cuber, p. 143.)

One of my favorite quotations about conflicts in relationships comes from Luke 17:1-4. It simply states, "It is impossible but that offences will come" and then goes on to give a beautiful rule about forgiveness. Perhaps, then, we should not be overwhelmed that conflicts do occur in marriage. The key is what we do with them when they arise.

Horribilizing

Sometimes when we do encounter what may be only minor conflicts in marriage, we make more out of them than

110

we should. Dr. Albert Ellis calls this "horribilizing." Do you "horribilize" in your marriage? Most of us do, placing unnecessary tensions and burdens on our relationship. What is horribilizing? Simply put, it is making a difficult or bad situation worse by irrational thought. It is making mountains out of molehills.

You recall the story of the traveling salesman who had a flat tire on his car one night out in the country. He got out of his car to change the flat tire, only to discover he had left his jack at home. The salesman saw a farmhouse in the distance and decided to go there to borrow a jack from the farmer.

While he was walking to the farmhouse, he began thinking, "It's late at night, and the farmer will probably be upset that I got him out of bed." The salesman walked a little ways farther and thought, "He'll probably think I'm really stupid traveling without a jack in my car." As he approached the farmhouse, he muttered to himself, "The farmer is probably stingy and won't loan me a jack even for a few minutes."

With that in mind he angrily knocked on the door. A light came on in the kitchen, and the farmer in pajamas opened the door. Without warning, the salesman reached in and punched the farmer in the mouth, shouting, "Keep your blankety-blank jack!"

The salesman may not have known it, but he was a horribilizer. Through irrational thought he made a difficult or bad situation worse, both for him and the unsuspecting farmer. Carlfred Broderick states, "To horribilize is to translate the undeniable fact that it is disappointing not to have things go your way into the idea that it is awful, terrible, and horrible that things are not different. Once you have convinced yourself that some situation is unfair, unbearable, and intolerable, you are all set up for depression, headaches, ulcers, and other symptoms of anxiety and tension. Being a horribilizer is *not* very rewarding." (Broderick, *Marriage*, p. 83.)

Susan and I found this out not long ago when we faced a very difficult day. We knew it was coming because of the list of things we had to do: We both had extremely busy

111

schedules the next day; our children had to be taken places; people were coming to do some last minute touch-ups on our new home; and two of our children were ill. In order to meet the heavy demands, everything would have to fit into a tight schedule. Everyone would have to meet their obligations on time, with no additional infringements on our time and energy.

The day arrived. I woke up at 5:30 A.M. and groaned, "It's here. The day has begun!" I moaned and rolled over in bed. "Nothing will probably go right. It will just be one of those days."

Susan was now awake. "You're probably right," she said. "Today is going to be exhausting. The repairmen will probably be late, and I won't get to my appointment on time." She paused and then asked, "Have you checked with the children to see if they're any better?"

"No, they're probably worse. That will complicate the day even more."

"I just don't know how we're going to make it," Susan commented as she went to shower. I lay in bed trying to figure out how to survive what obviously would be a difficult and trying day.

By 6:30 A.M. we were both dressed . . . and fatigued—and the day hadn't even begun. We continued to commiserate for a few more minutes. Then we stopped.

"Do you know what we're doing right now?" I asked.

"No, what?" she responded.

"We're horribilizing."

"We're what?"

"We are making a difficult day worse. The day hasn't even begun, yet here we are nearly out of energy."

We thought over our past hour, and then we began to laugh. Yes, we did have a busy and hectic day ahead, but by allowing our thoughts, attention, and conversation to wander aimlessly and dwell upon our troubles, we had made our day infinitely worse than it might have been. Our day turned out to be hectic, to say the least, but it was much less so than if we had continued to horribilize.

Remember the salesman, the farmer, and the jack the next time you begin to horribilize. Bad situations are often made worse by irrational and uncontrolled thinking.

Marital Pinches

When was the last time you pinched your husband or wife? Did you hurt them? Did it cause some irritation on their part? There are some experts on marriage today who believe that many marital problems arise over marital "pinches"—not the kind involving physical pain but the small or minor irritations that often arise in relationships between husbands and wives.

One article in the November 1984 issue of *Marriage Enrichment* newsletter talks about marital "pinches." ("Act on a Pinch," p. 5.) The editors believe that a major crisis in marriage almost always results from a series of small irritations (marital pinches) that are not dealt with when they arise. The article suggests that these minor areas of stress be confronted and discussed as they arise before they become major events. Perhaps the quality of the marital relationship is largely determined by whether, and how, married couples regularly and faithfully "act on a pinch."

What are some examples of marital pinches? The article lists quite a few of them as developed by Marcy and Ralph Reed:

—You forgot to tell me about the meeting you have at 7:30 P.M.

—You talk to me while I am on the telephone.

—You leave a mess in the bathroom.

—You talk to me from another room.

—You don't ask me what is wrong when you know that something is wrong.

—You make light of a problem I tell you about.

—You use up all the gas in the car.

—You come home from work and yell at the children because you are tired.

—You remind me of something stupid I did five years ago.

—You are often not ready on time.

—You sometimes pay more attention to the newspaper or the TV than to me.

—You repeat something which I have told you in confidence.

—While I'm talking, you walk away and do something else.

—You forget to do something I asked you to do.

—You start a job but you don't finish it.

—You tease me about my cooking in front of others.

—You keep putting off that weekend alone you promised we would take.

—You question my judgment in front of the children.

Have you been or do you become slightly irritated over these or other seemingly minor matters? If so, you were pinched.

The article on marital pinches suggests the following exercise. When you are both feeling relatively well and calm, talk about your marital pinches. You may want to review the preceding list together to see if some of these occur in your marriage. Take turns talking and listening. Then develop a policy for dealing with these pinches when they occur in the future.

Perhaps infrequent, accidental pinches should be tolerated and forgotten, but many pinches, particularly in the same area, should be discussed. Several small pinches can hurt and be highly irritating. Would your marriage improve if you learned to deal with the pinches? If you did, you would be following some seasoned advice given hundreds of years ago: "Moreover if thy brother [or spouse] shall trespass against thee, go and tell him his fault between thee and him alone: if he shall hear thee, thou hast gained thy brother." (Matt. 18:15.)

114

The Four Cs of Conflict Resolution

Marital conflict might be simply defined as "a clash of wishes," for it is nearly impossible to imagine any couple who would always want or wish for exactly the same thing in their marriage, no matter how much they love each other. But what do you do when conflict occurs? There are at least four approaches, the four Cs, that a couple can use to deal with marital conflict. They are (1) *coexist*, (2) *capitulate*, (3) *compromise*, and (4) *collaborate*.

1. *Coexist* (Accommodate). (See Mace, *Close*, p. 105.)

Person A   Person B

Simply put, a couple should learn to live with some conflicts in marriage. Not all conflicts can or should be resolved—a couple just agrees to disagree. A couple may differ in their food preferences, political philosophy, or hobbies and yet not have those differences affect their marital relationship negatively. One time I spoke to a group and made the statement that a good marriage is not determined by how much a husband and wife are alike but by how many differences they can tolerate in each other. After I had finished, one woman came up and said the thought was quite interesting. She said she had struggled for years with the concept of being one. Because she and her husband had so many differences, she felt they would never attain the goal of oneness. During our seminar, however, we had discussed how two people who tolerate each other's differences can actually become emotionally closer than those who constantly fight the differences.

Some conflicts in marriage are minor and do not merit massive amounts of time, emotion, or money in trying to resolve them. Coexistence is a good strategy in these cases. Each election year Susan and I have gone to the voting polls and cancelled each other's vote by voting for different candidates. Seldom have we agreed. Somehow, though, our marriage has managed to survive this and other areas of differences.

2. *Capitulate* (Acquiesce). (See Mace, *Close*, p. 102.)

Person A   ⟶   Person B

or

Person A   ⟵   Person B

In this method of conflict resolution one person "gives in" or adopts the other's position or point of view. He or she simply yields. This approach is obviously disadvantageous if one person is continually yielding or acquiescing to the other. However, when both marriage partners are willing to yield on occasion for the sake of the marriage, capitulation is a useful and effective approach.

There are two types of capitulation. In one, a spouse gives in because of coercion or forced submission. In the other, a spouse gives in because of caring, persuasion, long-suffering, gentleness, meekness, or love unfeigned. (See D&C 121:41.) The latter type of capitulation is the desirable one.

Susan and I, for example, differ in our likes and dislikes of movies. She likes the more romantic, emotionally involving stories while I like the action-packed stories. When we decide to go to a movie, we usually have to use the second C, *Capitulate*, by one giving in to the other. I must admit that I have slept through more than one tearjerker, but I do enjoy going with her. And as the occasion arises, she goes with me to the more adventure-filled movies. During our marriage we have found we both like James Bond films, and lately I have stayed awake long enough to shed a tear or two during her movies. But neither one minds giving in, on occasion, to the other because we know that our marriage is more important than what movies we go to see.

3. *Compromise* (Negotiate). (See Mace, *Close*, p. 104.)

Person A   ⟶   ⟵   Person B

116

With the third C, *Compromise*, spouses yield or give in until they find a middle ground or devise an alternative solution. I honestly feel that almost all differences that cause conflict in marriage can be negotiated. An example might be which parents a newly wedded couple will visit on Thanksgiving or Christmas. Sometimes visiting both sets of parents is difficult if not impossible, so a couple will arrange to visit one set of parents one year and the other the next. Or they might go to one place for Thanksgiving and the other for Christmas. (The example may sound trite, but it is a common situation with recently married couples.)

I remember my mother and father had one minor conflict over food. Dad enjoyed eating beef liver, but Mom literally became ill at the smell of it being cooked. So they negotiated the conflict. On the day—usually a Saturday—that Dad wanted beef liver, Mom would go shopping. Dad agreed to cook it himself, have all the dishes done, and air out the kitchen sufficiently before she returned. Minor conflict—excellent negotiation.

Other areas of conflict that might be negotiated are recreational and musical preferences (bowlers married to opera buffs, for example), amounts of personal spending money, household tasks, and even some aspects of sexual relationships. Negotiation and compromise have their advantages and disadvantages. Among the latter is that neither spouse totally receives what he or she wants. But the advantage is that both get some of what they want. Through skilled negotiation, most marital conflicts can be resolved or significantly modified.

4. *Collaborate* (Win/win).

Person A   ⟶   Goal

Person B   ⟶   Goal

To collaborate means "to work with another or others" and, I would add, "until both derive their major goals." In all

117

other methods of conflict resolution mentioned thus far, at least one spouse, and sometimes both, needs to give in to some extent. In the collaboration approach both husband and wife would state their desires, goals, or ambitions. Then, if possible, both would set out to assist the other in attaining their desires. Suppose the husband wants a relatively expensive camera and the wife wants a new, also expensive, grandfather clock for the hallway. They could (1) coexist with each other's desires and do nothing; (2) capitulate so one gives in to the other—either the husband gets the camera, or the wife gets the grandfather clock; (3) compromise so the husband gets a less expensive camera and the wife settles for a clock for the fireplace mantle; or (4) collaborate so both work for what the other desires—he gets the camera he wants, and she gets her grandfather clock.

Perhaps they could collaborate by selling something they own. Maybe they could earn the extra money through a second job for one or through a joint money-raising project. Whatever the strategy, both would work, plan, and persist until the joint goals are reached. Granted, the collaboration approach to conflict has its limitations and may not be practical in all marriage situations, but it is one that can satisfy both partners fully and bring them closer together. Couples should consider using collaboration whenever the situation allows.

How to Get Out of the Turmoil Trap

In my marriage enhancement classes at BYU, I give the students an assignment titled "Dealing with Differences." We first discuss the following sequence: Differences ◊ Disagreements ◊ Conflict ◊ Anger. During the week that follows, married couples are to write down all the differences they can think of in their marriage. Then, after they have both contributed to the list, they are to put them into two separate categories: essential and nonessential differences.

Nonessential differences are those differences that arise in marriage that really should not affect the stability of the marriage or the satisfaction of the marriage partners. Essential differences are those differences that do matter, in which one or both have some vested interest.

We then discuss the following statement by B. H. Roberts: "In essentials let there be unity; in non-essentials, liberty; and in all things, charity." (Roberts, p. 30.)

By this time we have found some interesting results. Most of the differences they have identified usually turn out to be nonessential differences, and only a few can be identified as essential differences. In addition, I point out to the students that differences need not lead to disagreements if we can agree to disagree and realize that some differences are normal in any given marriage. We also talk about anger (the topic of the next chapter, "Trap 8: The Temper Trap").

Finally, we look over our list of differences, both essential and nonessential, and determine how the four Cs might be applied to each of the areas of potential conflict.

Where can we *coexist* and just practice tolerance and patience? In what areas might we *capitulate*, simply acquiescing to our husbands or wives by giving in? Which areas of conflict could we settle if we *compromise*, that is, negotiate or bargain for a mutually agreeable solution? And finally, when will it be possible to *collaborate*, or try for the win-win strategy in which both spouses work to help each other attain what he or she is seeking?

By applying the four Cs of conflict resolution, we can deal with marital conflict adequately and constructively when it does arise. And by working to resolve the conflicts in our marriages, we will hopefully never have to encounter or even discuss the fifth C of conflict resolution . . . that of *cancellation*, or divorce.

| TRAP 8 |
| THE |
| TEMPER |
| TRAP |
| |

Temper: State of feeling or frame of mind usually dominated by a single strong emotion; heat of mind or emotion, proneness to anger, passion.

THE TEMPER TRAP: *The inability or unwillingness of marriage partners to control, modify, or possibly eliminate anger in their relationship.*

O ne of the interesting paradoxes in marriage is that marriage partners who love each other sometimes become highly irritated or annoyed with each other. On occasion there may be outright anger. It would be meaningless to debate whether a person should or should not become angry at someone they love; the fact is, they often do. Sometimes a spouse will do something over which his or her marriage partner becomes upset. On occasion, the absence of action or words may also irritate the spouse. There are both sins of omission and sins of commission in provoking anger.

Recall for a moment the last time you became angry at your spouse or someone else you dearly love. What was the situation? What happened to trigger your anger? What did the other person say or do? Most important, how were you feeling about yourself before the incident occurred?

Apparently anger and irritation are frequently linked to one's self-esteem. Husbands or wives often become irritated and upset with their spouses when they are angry at themselves. In this regard, Dr. Albert Ellis and Dr. Robert Harper, psychotherapists from Washington, D.C., and New York have reported in their book, *A Guide to Successful Marriage*, that "there is an all too human tendency for us to get irritated with others in direct proportion to our irritation with ourselves." (Ellis, p. 79.)

If the observation of Drs. Ellis and Harper is correct, and I believe it is, we learn at least two important concepts about anger and marriage. First, if our spouses are angry or upset, they may not be living up to their expectations at that time, and their self-esteem may be low because of some supposed or real failures. Their anger or hostility may have nothing to do with the marriage even though it is vented on the nearest person available. Thus realizing this, we could check our first assumption that the anger is directed at us, and we would be better able to keep ourselves from retaliation. Realizing the cause of anger should make us more capable of controlling our own responses.

Second, we should be more careful about not projecting our hostility toward our loved ones. If we find ourselves misdirecting our anger, we should retract our angry statements immediately and apologize for our behavior, admitting that we are actually upset with ourselves and not with our spouses.

I have a friend who once told me about a large tree a few blocks from his home. Each evening as he drives home, he stops by the tree and examines his emotional state. He does not want to bring the problems of work to his marriage and family, and stopping by the large tree is a reminder not to do so. This has helped him avoid the Farmer-in-the-Dell syndrome, a phenomenon in many marriages and families that deals with displaced irritations and anger.

The Farmer-in-the-Dell syndrome works like this: A person has a bad day, and self-esteem approaches zero. Suppose the husband is experiencing this. He arrives home in a discouraged state and says something to his wife that reflects his irritation. She then assumes he is angry at her, and her ill feelings mount. The wife then says something to the oldest child that indicates her annoyance, and the oldest child then crabs at the next oldest. This irritation is passed from child to child until it reaches the youngest one, who, having no one else to turn on, attacks the family cat. Such is displaced anger, which we have all seen or noticed in one form or another in our marriages and families.

What Is Your I.Q.?

Both the Bible and the Book of Mormon admonish that we should not be "easily provoked." (1 Cor. 13:5; Moro. 7:45.) But are we easily irritated? And more importantly, are we easily angered? Here is a little test to help you determine your I.Q., or Irritability Quotient. The test and scoring method have been adapted from the Novaco Provocation Inventory developed by Dr. R. W. Novaco.

Read over the list of twenty-five potentially upsetting

situations. Then, in the space provided, estimate the degree of your response with the following measurement:

0 - I would feel very little or no annoyance.
1 - I would feel a little irritated.
2 - I would feel moderately upset.
3 - I would feel quite angry.
4 - I would feel very angry.

For example, on question 4, "You get your car stuck in the mud or snow," if you believe "I would feel moderately upset," you would write a 2 in the space provided.

Scale

____ 1. You unpack an appliance you have just bought, plug it in, and discover that it doesn't work.

____ 2. You are overcharged by a repairman who has you in a bind.

____ 3. You are singled out for correction when the actions of others go unnoticed.

____ 4. You get your car stuck in the mud or snow.

____ 5. You are talking to someone who doesn't answer you.

____ 6. Someone pretends to be something he or she is not.

____ 7. While you are struggling to carry four sodas to your table at a cafeteria, someone bumps into you, spilling the sodas.

____ 8. You have hung up your clothes, but someone knocks them to the floor and fails to pick them up.

____ 9. You are hounded by a salesman from the moment you walk into a store.

____ 10. You have made arrangements to go somewhere, but the person backs out at the last minute and leaves you all alone.

____ 11. You are being joked about or teased.

____ 12. Your car is stalled at a traffic light, and the guy behind you keeps blowing his horn.

____ 13. You accidentally make the wrong kind of turn in a parking lot. As you get out of the car, someone yells at you, "Where did you learn to drive?"

____ 14. Someone makes a mistake and blames it on you.

124

___ 15. You are trying to concentrate, but a person near you is tapping his or her foot.

___ 16. You lend someone an important book or tool, and he or she fails to return it.

___ 17. You have had a busy day, and the person you live with complains that you forgot to do something you agreed to do.

___ 18. You are trying to discuss something important with your mate or partner, who isn't giving you a chance to express your feelings.

___ 19. You are in a discussion with someone who persists in arguing about a topic he or she knows very little about.

___ 20. Someone intrudes and interrupts an argument between you and someone else.

___ 21. You need to get somewhere quickly, but the car in front of you is going 25 mph in a 40 mph zone, and you can't pass.

___ 22. You step on a wad of chewing gum.

___ 23. You are mocked by a small group of people as you pass them.

___ 24. In a hurry to get somewhere, you tear a good pair of slacks on a sharp object.

___ 25. You use your last coin to make a phone call, but you are disconnected before you finish dialing, and the money is lost.

After completing the evaluation, you can determine your Irritability Quotient. Make sure you answered all the questions, and then simply add up the score for the twenty-five situations.

The lowest score would be *0* while the highest would be *100*. Few attain either of these scores. Here is a possible explanation of your I.Q.

    0-45 The amount of anger and annoyance you generally experience is remarkably low.

  46-55 You respond with less anger than most people in irritating situations.

  56-75 You respond about average to life's annoyances.

  76-85 You respond with substantially more anger

than average to irritating experiences in life. You are a fairly irritable person.

86-100   You have a very high I.Q. and frequently encounter intense reactions that do not go away quickly. You probably harbor negative feelings and likely experience frequent headaches and high blood pressure. Relatively few people respond to anger as intently as do you.

Anger Is Controversial

I have found the topic of anger to be somewhat controversial with some couples, particularly among Latter-day Saints. I often ask the question, "Do you ever become angry at your husband or wife?" Some will say "yes." Others will not reply. I then rephrase my question, "Do you ever become irritated with your marriage partner?" At this point, most couples will nod their heads in agreement. Many married couples feel that people who love each other should never be angry with each other. If they do become angry, they supposedly do not love each other. Hence, many are unwilling to admit anger or even slight annoyances with their spouses.

Several years ago I had the opportunity of talking to Dr. David Mace at a family life conference in Portland, Oregon. He and his wife, Vera, were then in their seventies and about to retire from full-time involvement in marriage enrichment and counseling. They were also about to take semiretirement from the management of a group they had started called ACME: Association of Couples for Marriage Enrichment. They had been involved in these areas for over fifty years and have probably done more good than any other couple to promote stability and satisfaction in contemporary marriage in the United States.

On the occasion of their semiretirement, Dr. Mace made an interesting observation. After more than fifty years of counseling and marriage enrichment involvement, he said that if he had only one hour to help a couple do something to improve their marriage, he would help them learn to deal with anger. He said that when people are angry, they usually are not loving. Anger conceals, even if momentarily, loving and caring feelings. If couples allow themselves to be continually angry, they will not allow themselves or their spouses the opportunity to be loving. Love and anger, he claimed, are two sides of the same coin in human relationships. The irony is that we often become the most angry or irritated with those individuals we love the most.

Since that time Dr. Mace has written a book titled *Love & Anger in Marriage* (Grand Rapids, Michigan: Zondervan Publishing House, 1982.) It can be purchased in many Christian bookstores or may be ordered from ACME, 459 S. Church Street, P.O. Box 10596, Winston-Salem, N.C. 27108. I highly recommend the book.

Here is one of Dr. Mace's observations from *Love & Anger in Marriage:*

> During a lifetime of working as a professional in the field of marriage and the family, I have eagerly sought to understand the immense complexity of close interpersonal relationships. And I have often asked myself whether there might be one key issue that would explain why so many marriages, embarked upon with such high hopes, finally falter and fail. In time an answer began to emerge. First in my own marriage, and then in the marriages of many other couples whom I sought to help, the management of anger seemed to be especially important. As I continued to explore what I called *the love-anger cycle,* I became convinced that I had tracked down the critical issue. (Mace, *Love,* pp. 9-10.)

Here are four of his premises:

1. The state of marriage generates in normal people more anger than they are likely to experience in any other type of relationship in which they habitually find themselves. . . .

2. Unless the anger thus generated can be processed as raw material for the development for intimacy, the possibility of closeness in the relationship is denied. The love and

warmth that are sought in it fail to develop, and a sense of disillusionment results that can easily lead to alienation.

3. The underlying cause of this widespread alienation [between spouses and family members] is the fact that the persons concerned do not understand, and therefore are not able to process productively, the anger that is generated in their intimate interactions. The methods they use to deal with their anger are counterproductive.

4. It is possible, however, though not easy, to learn new skills which foster a more productive and creative use of anger so that it will reinforce, instead of destroy, love and intimacy. (Mace, *Love*, pp. 12-13.)

Dr. Mace describes several ways individuals deal with anger. There is (1) *fight*, the physical and emotional confrontation or attack on the perceived source of threat; (2) *flight*, the running away from an opponent or situation that seems to be overpowering; (3) *freeze*, the "do nothing" or "play dead" approach where those confronted see the situation as hopeless; and (4) *relax*, the relaxation of muscles and physical tension after the brain sends the message to the body that the threat is over. This might be done spontaneously (a false alarm) or by conscious choice when the threat is less than that originally perceived. (See Mace, *Love*, pp. 33-37.) He notes that many couples, particularly newlyweds, often are disillusioned to find that they do become angry at someone they love.

Three Perspectives of Anger

To help understand the topic of anger better, let's assume there are three different perspectives toward anger:

Perspective 1: Anger is an instinctive response to threat. Therefore, neither the onset nor the consequences of anger can be controlled.

Perspective 2: Anger is an instinctive response to threat, but we are in control of what we do about our anger.

Perspective 3: We can choose whether or not we are going to become (or remain) angry, and we may therefore choose not to experience the consequences of anger.

Let's examine each perspective more closely. Perspective 1 (no control of origin or consequences) is something like a temper tantrum. It gives one an excuse for becoming angry because the individual is supposedly not responsible for the anger. When we say things like "you make me so angry that I . . ." we are operating from Perspective 1. Those who advocate this belief claim our physical makeup is such that we spontaneously respond to threatening situations. Anger, therefore, supposedly protects both body and ego.

Perspective 2 suggests that, while we cannot on occasion help becoming angry, we can do something about it once we do become angry. This philosophy is suggested in the biblical verse, "Be ye angry, and sin not: let not the sun go down upon your wrath." (Eph. 4:26.) Latter-day Saints may be interested in Joseph Smith's revision of that scripture, "Can ye be angry, and not sin?" which has a different connotation. Dr. Mace, in *Love & Anger in Marriage*, takes a Perspective 2 position. He claims that we will, on occasion, become angry even with loved ones. His approach is that anger is normal, and normal people become angry.

Perspective 3 is a little more difficult but, I believe, mature approach to anger. It simply views anger as a choice. We can decide or choose whether or not we become angry. By choosing not to become angry, we can avoid all the negative consequences that attend anger.

Burton C. Kelly, in the February 1980 *Ensign*, discusses Perspective 3. He claims that, though we will not all immediately develop the ability to choose or refuse anger, as long as we know it is possible, it becomes attainable. Brother Kelly states, "Few of us reach adulthood without experiencing anger—our own or someone else's. In fact, society seems to tell us that occasional anger is inevitable and normal, even healthy. I believe, however, that anger is not only unhealthy and harmful, but can be eliminated. A few basic ideas about the nature of anger can help us see the gospel answer to purging anger entirely from our lives, thus taking a giant step toward the charity and self-control we all seek to develop."

Burton Kelly then states and gives a rationale for *each* of four basic principles:

1. We are ultimately responsible for our own anger.
2. Anger between individuals is the result of sin.
3. Anger itself is a sin when sin is defined as anything that retards the growth or progress of an individual.
4. Anger usually has harmful interpersonal consequences—it often results in injury to the self-esteem and dignity of another, and/or erosion of mutual respect.

Brother Kelly also defines the difference between the Lord's anger and that of mortals. In addition, he gives several "gospel cures" for anger, such as dealing with it quickly, having faith in our capability not to become angry, and developing knowledge—through awareness, self-discipline, and forgiveness. He says that many people ask him if he still becomes angry. His reply:

> Unfortunately, yes. But not as often, not as intensely, and not for as long. When I stop and consider these principles, my anger fades away. . . . I try to remember that my anger is a signal that I need to correct some of my thoughts (those that induced it), that it is a reminder of weaknesses *I* need to overcome.
>
> I realize that the goal of eliminating anger is a tremendous challenge—and not one to be conquered in a single step—but I testify that as we strive to do so we will not only markedly improve our own relationships with others and increase in joy and happiness, but also enjoy better health, more energy, and more vitality. Further, as we conquer anger we will prepare ourselves to help others eliminate the destructiveness of anger from their lives. . . .
>
> I also believe that we will not really know the blessing nor the purpose of living this commandment until we have lived it. The full blessings and understanding come *after* having lived the commandment, not before (see Moses 5: 6-8). (Kelly, pp. 9-13.)

The Gospel Is the Key to Resolving Anger

Terrance D. Olson, in the August 1982 *Ensign*, states, "I am convinced that the gospel of Jesus Christ is the solution—

a very practical one—to problems in marriage. Even though some husbands and wives see scriptural counsel as too 'abstract' or too 'idealistic,' I see continually how the gospel is the source of personal and marital happiness and that it has the answers to solving problems in marriage."

He then gives a specific example:

> Our hostile feelings toward another person are more fundamental to our problems than that person's behavior. What others do to us does not render us uncompassionate or unforgiving. We do that to ourselves by refusing to forgive. Our road to personal peace requires our own repentance of those feelings of resentment. Consider Doctrine and Covenants 64:10: "I, the Lord, will forgive whom I will forgive, but of you it is required to forgive all men."
>
> An attitude of forgiveness toward our companion is an important beginning. By having faith in the first two commandments, we are blessed by them. By loving the Lord with all our heart, we see our situation differently. By loving our husband or wife as ourselves, we see him or her more compassionately, and are no longer in despair. We are traveling on a gospel road, rather than on a path which denies the gospel. . . .
>
> The gospel teaches us that we are free to "act for [ourselves] and not be acted upon, . . . and all things are given [us] which are expedient." (2 Ne. 2:26-27.) In other words, whatever our spouse's attitudes or sins might be, his or her behavior is not sufficient to render us incapable of living as we feel we should.

Terrance Olson's article, "The Compassionate Marriage Partner," which relates the gospel to marriage, should be read in its entirety. (Olson, pp. 14-17.)

Tim LaHaye and Bob Phillips have also written a fine book on Christian methods of resolving anger, *Anger Is a Choice* (Grand Rapids, Michigan: Zondervan Publishing House, 1982). This book is available in most Christian bookstores. Latter-day Saints will appreciate its scriptural insight into anger through numerous references to biblical verses. Particularly helpful are the chapters "Is It Ever Right to Be

Angry?" "Anger and Forgiveness," "Anger in the Bible," and "How to Deal with Your Anger."

How to Get Out of the Temper Trap

Like other traps described in this book, the temper trap is not easy to escape. The first step, however, is to realize that you are in it. Do you have a high Irritability Quotient? Then do a lot of study of articles and books such as those suggested—give yourself to much introspection and praying, and discuss the problem with your spouse. Professional counseling might also be sought. If we are, as the scriptures say, "easily provoked" (1 Cor. 13:5 and Moro. 7:45), we do not yet have the pure love of Christ.

In my marriage classes and seminars I suggest that married couples closely examine the three perspectives of anger and decide two things: (1) which perspective are they now using, and (2) which perspective would they like to use? I feel successful if we move any person or couple from Perspective 1 to Perspective 2 or 3. I also suggest that they keep an Anger Log for two weeks and experiment with the idea that anger can be a choice. Can we actually choose to be or to not be angry?

An Anger Log is a notebook or journal that a person keeps for fourteen days. During that time he or she records all the "opportunities" for anger and the attendant results. Did he or she respond with Perspective 1, 2, or 3 in each of the situations? If the person is one of my students, at the end of the two-week period, I collect the log with its personal comments and observations.

Interestingly, few couples ever make it for the full two weeks without becoming angry (or "very annoyed" as they put it) at their marriage partners. But they report that they are amazed how often they do exercise control over situations when they heretofore would have just let themselves go emotionally.

During a marriage enhancement course at BYU one semester, I gave the Anger Log assignment and then volunteered to do it myself for two weeks. I was to report back to the students my successes or failures. The class ended, and the students left. My car was being repaired that afternoon, so I phoned Susan and asked her to pick me up at a designated location outside my office. She said she would be there at 4:30 P.M.

I went outside my office about that time and began waiting. It started raining but I decided to wait because she surely would be by soon. Five minutes went by. Then ten and fifteen. Soon it was 5:00 P.M. and no Susan. During that time I started fuming inside. Why would she leave me waiting in the rain? Surely I had a reason to be angry. She was late and had no reason to *make me* stand there in the rain and wait. I felt the anger starting to mount. A young married couple from my marriage class walked by. Even though it was raining, they stopped to say they had enjoyed the discussion on anger. They also reminded me of the assignment we had all agreed upon little more than an hour earlier. They added that they were interested in hearing about my Anger Log.

I decided I should not fail within sixty minutes of the assignment, so I resolved not to become angry!

Susan finally arrived at 5:05 P.M. I wish I could have photographed the look on her face as I climbed into the car, glasses foggy and water dripping off the rims.

"Go ahead and say it," she said as she bristled.

"Say what?" I replied in a mild-mannered Clark Kent voice.

"Say something about my being 35 minutes late."

"Well, I really didn't enjoy standing in the rain that long."

"I thought a college professor would have enough sense to go back inside the building once it started raining," she said, still on guard.

"I simply decided not to become angry," I revealed rather flamboyantly. I then told her about the assignment and my agreement to participate.

Susan sat in the driver's seat, car motor still running, and then exclaimed, "This is nothing short of a miracle!"

133

I soon found out that a real estate agent had brought by a couple to look at our home for sale. She knew, and we both agreed, that the wait was warranted, and the incident was soon set aside.

In case you are wondering, no, I didn't make it for the full two weeks without becoming angry. I did survive a cracked window that week. (I congratulated our nine-year-old son on his enthusiasm for baseball.) But then during the second weekend, our family of eight (at that time six children) decided to take a long drive in the family station wagon. The afternoon got hot, the kids started fighting over space, my nerves wore thin, and . . . need I say more? I forgot about my assignment and the Anger Log and let myself retrogress to Perspective 1 during one of their encounters. But neither their fight nor my anger lasted long, so perhaps there is still hope.

During education week at BYU one summer, I challenged nearly one thousand people to try the Anger Log for only one week. A wife later wrote and told me what miraculous things had happened in their marriage. Her husband, a construction supervisor, angered easily but decided he would try the Anger Log for one week. She said it was marvelous while it lasted. But he, like myself, didn't make it the full time. She said he worked at it for six days, but on the seventh he rested.

Try the Anger Log for two weeks. See if you can do any better than her husband or yours truly.

Can anger be a choice? Interesting thought, and worthwhile pursuit.

TRAP 9

THE
TENSION
TRAP

Tension: Mental or emotional strain; suspense, anxiety, or excitement; pressure.

THE TENSION TRAP: *Participation in too many stress-producing projects or activities.*

I don't know if your marriage is like ours, but it seems that my wife and I undergo a great deal of tension. Some of it is external and comes from without with little or no control over its origin. We can only try to counter it when it occurs. Perhaps we all need to better understand the admonition that "it is not requisite that a man should run faster than he has strength." (Mosiah 4:27. See also D&C 10:4.)

Susan and I often experience stress when we begin projects and take a long time in finishing them. But we are learning. One of the most stressful experiences in our marriage occurred several years ago. We were living in Wisconsin and decided that our house needed a coat of paint. A paint contractor gave us a bid of $500 to complete the job. We later figured that if we painted it ourselves, we could save about $200. So with very good intentions we set about to do so.

Spring arrived as we began our house-painting project. It was warm weather, so we cheerfully began painting. There was a pitcher of iced Kool-Aid on the patio table. It was a scene worthy of a Norman Rockwell painting. But about that time the pleasant part ended. After starting, we learned that the old paint had to be scraped off, which took much more time and work than we had anticipated. We would also have to apply a primer coat, which we had not known about.

About that time we found out that Susan was pregnant with our fifth child. Consequently, she became nauseated with the smell of paint. In addition, at the university where I was teaching summer school, some unexpected projects developed that also required a great deal of time and effort.

Very quickly, our house-painting project to save $200 began to drag on and on, and the tension started to build. We started scraping and painting one end of the house, and as time passed on, the unfinished work remained as a monument to our inability to finish a major project we had started. Our painting project, or the lack of it, became the object of many good-natured jokes with our neighbors.

As the spring weather began to disappear, so did our patience, first with our project, then with each other. Each afternoon as I arrived home from the university, the unfinished, unpainted house stood there to greet me defiantly as I drove in the driveway.

After dinner one evening, I knew I was supposed to go out and either scrape, prime, or paint. But I was exhausted. So Susan and I sat down and reexamined the situation. We recalled the original bid of $500 for the professional painter to come and paint our house. We had been sincere in wanting to save $200 by painting it ourselves. But in the process we realized that the project had become a major source of contention in our marriage. We both agreed that our marriage was worth more to us than $200.

So the next day we went down to the credit union, borrowed the $500, and called the painter. It was one of the wisest things we ever did, and one of the best investments we ever made in our marriage. We were able to go on and enjoy what otherwise would have been a very frustrating summer. Plus, the professional painter did a much better job on our house than we would have done.

It often amazes me how much money people will justify for borrowing or spending on items of personal interest, but when it comes to borrowing or spending money to avoid something that is a source of contention in a marriage, what penny-pinchers we become. Exactly how much money is a marriage worth anyway?

Learn a lesson from Brent and Susan Barlow. Be careful not to begin projects you can't finish. Does that sound like original advice? It isn't. We read it first in the Bible. Several hundred years ago Jesus Christ taught, "For which of you, intending to build a tower, sitteth not down first, and counteth the cost, whether he have sufficient to finish it? Lest haply, after he hath laid the foundation, and is not able to finish it, all that behold it begin to mock him, saying, This man began to build, and was not able to finish." (Luke 14:28-30.)

137

A Time of Chaos

Children can also be a source of tension in contemporary married life. About the time we think we have everything under control, life becomes more hectic.

In 1983 I sat down with paper and pencil in hand and began to outline the history of our marriage. It seemed to fall into distinct periods, and I thought if I ever wrote about it, the outline would be something like this:

Chapter One: "Beginnings, 1965-1968." We were married on June 5, 1965, and during the first year I attended BYU to complete my bachelor's degree. Susan taught at Cherry Hill Elementary School in Orem while I finished my senior year. The following two years we lived in Kaysville, Utah, where I taught LDS Seminary at Davis High School and finished my master's degree. Doug was born in 1967.

Chapter Two: "Preparation, 1968-1971." During this time we moved to Tallahassee, Florida, where I worked on my Ph.D. at Florida State University. Tammy was born in 1969 and Brian in 1971 in Florida. The pace of life picked up.

Chapter Three: "Establishment, 1971-1977." For the next three years we lived in Carbondale, Illinois, and then in Eau Claire, Wisconsin, for another three years. I taught at Southern Illinois University and then at the University of Wisconsin-Stout. Jon was born in Illinois in 1973, and Jason was born in Wisconsin in 1976. We were into parenthood full swing.

Chapter Four: "Chaos, 1977-1983." During these six years we moved to Utah, where I began teaching at Brigham Young University. Kris was born in 1980, the three older children moved into their teens, Susan began teaching parttime, and I began to write a newspaper column and books about marriage. It seemed like we were all going a hundred miles an hour in different directions. About this same time we realized that our house was too small, so we commenced plans for a new, larger house.

After outlining chapter four, "Chaos," I became a bit philosophical. We had all our children, I thought, with the oldest nearly seventeen and the youngest moving up on four, so the worst of the hectic pace was behind us. Perhaps things would settle down, so I outlined the next chapter. Chapter Five, "Stability, 1983 and on." I was quite proud of my outline and called to Susan as she entered the house, "Please come here. I have something to show you."

"Yes, and I have something to tell you," she said as she came in and took off her coat.

"Look," I boasted as I showed her the outline history of our marriage, "don't you like the way I've divided it into five chapters?"

"What is this chapter five, 'Stability'?" she asked. "And what does it mean?"

"Well," I leaned back as I began, "I think that we are through the most difficult parts of parenting. We have our six children, and now all we have to do is let them grow up." Susan was quiet as she reviewed my outline.

"By the way, where have you been?" I asked.

"Oh, I had an appointment with the doctor."

"Is anything wrong?"

"No, not really." Then she paused. "We're going to have another baby!"

We were both quiet and reflective. After a few more moments of silence I said, "Maybe we had better cancel chapter five, 'Stability,' and continue chapter four, 'Chaos.'" She laughed and left the room.

It was Thanksgiving time, and I continued to reflect. We could still be thankful. We could still count our many blessings and name them one by one: Doug, Tammy, Brian, Jon, Jason, and Kris.

The following year, June 6, 1984, we added our seventh blessing. Brandon James Barlow was born. And at the time of the writing of this book, we are still in chapter four, "Chaos," with our many blessings, fast-paced life, and responsibilities.

Children Contribute to Tension

Since we were going to have another child, I realized I should be more supportive of Susan.

139

Not long ago I was talking to a friend of mine in Salt Lake City, Dr. Val MacMurray. Val shared with me an article he had recently co-authored with David C. Spendlove, M.S.W., and James R. Gaveleck, Ph.D., all of whom are affiliated with the University of Utah Medical Center. The article was titled "Learned Helplessness and the Depressed Housewife." The authors pointed out in their article that (as of 1978) 47 percent of the mothers in the United States who have children under the age of 18 do not work outside their homes for a salary. This figure "represents approximately 14.3 million women whose foremost responsibility is probably managing a household." Their research has particular relevance for married couples. They noted:

> One of the primary stresses on most housewives that helps account for both dependence and depression is child rearing. For several reasons, the demands of caring for children for most of the day leave the housewife more vulnerable than her employed husband to feelings of dependence. Having small children often means that a woman does not have time for adult contacts or time for being alone; moreover, the housewife who usually spends the majority of the day with her children may find them demanding of her time and effort in a manner that is not intellectually stimulating. Her husband, on the other hand, has the dual role of father and wage earner and not only receives emotional support at home, but often obtains a degree of intellectual stimulation at work. In addition, he has access to a network of social supports within the context of his job.
> A study by Brown and Harris recently found that women who had more than two children under the age of 14 were significantly more depressed than women who had fewer than two children, but that if the variable of number of children in the home was controlled . . . , women who worked were less depressed than those who did not. Merely working outside the home reduced by 50 percent the incidence of depression among the women included in the study who did not have a supportive relationship with a male companion. In the case of women who had such a

relationship, the number of children at home did not influence the development of depression. The implication one can draw from these findings is that women at home with more than two children need to have a supportive relationship with a male companion if they are to be relatively free from depression. Furthermore, the greater the number of young children a woman has, the more dependent she becomes on this key relationship. If a woman lacks such a relationship or is involved in a relationship that is not functioning well, the likelihood increases that she will feel depressed. (Spendlove, pp. 474-79.)

I once read a sign that said "A mother's place is in the home . . . and so is the father's!" And now we know why.

The Patti Perfect Syndrome

It is true that children contribute to tension and stress in a home. But many women, sometimes unknowingly, contribute to their own feelings of stress by trying to live a life-style that is unrealistic. Margaret B. Black and Midge W. Nielsen have, with tongue in cheek, noted this phenomenon among some LDS women in their article titled "Patti Perfect."

> *Many LDS women unconsciously compete with an idealized image of the already-perfect wife and mother who successfully incorporates all the demands of family, church, and society into her life. Although we have never met such a woman, we persist in believing she's out there somewhere. We can just imagine what she must accomplish in a day . . .*

Patti gets up very early and says her personal prayers. She zips her slim, vigorous body into her warmup suit and tiptoes outside to run her usual five miles (on Saturday she does ten). Returning home all aglow, she showers and dresses for the day in a tailored skirt and freshly starched and ironed blouse. She settles down for quiet meditation and scripture reading, before preparing the family breakfast. The morning's menu calls for whole wheat pancakes, homemade syrup, freshly squeezed orange juice, and powdered milk (the whole family loves it).

With classical music wafting through the air, Patti

141

awakens her husband and ten children. She spends a quiet moment with each and helps them plan a happy day. The children quickly dress in clothes that were laid out the night before. They cheerfully make their beds, clean their rooms, and do the individual chores assigned to them on the Family Work Wheel Chart. They assemble for breakfast the minute mother calls.

After family prayer and scripture study, the children all practice their different musical instruments. Father leaves for work on a happy note. All too soon it is time for the children to leave for school. Having brushed (and flossed) their teeth, the children pick up coats, book bags, and lunches which were prepared the night before and arrive at school five minutes early.

With things more quiet, Patti has story time with her pre-schoolers and teaches them a cognitive reading skill. She feeds, bathes, and rocks the baby before putting him down for his morning nap. With baby sleeping peacefully and the three-year-old twins absorbed in creative play, Patti tackles the laundry and housework. In less than an hour, everything is in order. Thanks to wise scheduling and children who are trained to work, her house never really gets dirty.

Proceeding to the kitchen, Patti sets out tonight's dinner: frozen veal parmigiana that she made in quantity from her home-grown tomatoes and peppers. She then mixes and kneads twelve loaves of bread. While the bread rises, Patti dips a batch of candles to supplement her food storage. As the bread bakes, she writes in her personal journal and dashes off a few quick letters: one to her Congressman and a couple of genealogy inquiries to distant cousins. Patti then prepares her mini-class on organic gardening. She also inserts two pictures and a certificate in little Paul's scrapbook, noting with satisfaction that all family albums are attractive and up-to-date. Checking the mail, Patti sees that their income tax refund has arrived—a result of having filed in January. It is earmarked for mission and college savings accounts. Although Patti's hardworking husband earns only a modest salary, her careful budgeting has kept the family debt-free.

After lunch, Patti drops the children off at Grandma's

for their weekly visit. Grandma enjoys babysitting and appreciates the warm loaf of bread. Making an extra call, Patti takes a second loaf to one of the sisters she is assigned to visit teach. A third loaf goes to the non-member neighbor on the corner.

Patti arrives at the elementary school where she directs a special education program. A clinical psychologist, Patti finds this an excellent way to stay abreast of her field while raising her family. Before picking up her little ones, Patti finishes collecting for the charity fund drive.

Home again, Patti settles the children down for their afternoon naps. She spends some quiet time catching up on her reading and filing. As she mists her luxuriant house plants, the school children come through the door. Patti listens attentively to each one as they tell her about their day. The children start right in on their homework, the mother supervising and encouraging them. When all schoolwork is done, Patti and the children enjoy working on one of their projects. Today they work on the quilt stretched on frames in a corner of the family room.

Dinnertime and father arrive, and it is a special hour for the whole family. They enjoy Patti's well-balanced, tasty meal, along with stimulating conversation. After dinner, father and the children pitch in to clean up so that mom can relax. She enjoys listening to the sounds of laughter and affection that come from the kitchen.

With the teenaged children in charge at home, mother and father attend an evening session at the Temple. During the return trip, they sit close together as in courting days. "Well dear," says Paul Perfect, "did you have a good day?" Patti reflectively answers, "Yes, I really did. But I feel I need more challenge in my life. I think I'll contact our Family Organization and volunteer to head up a reunion for August." (Black, p. 15.)

Although such a superwoman really does not exist, we recognize the model in the story because we have encountered many of the expectations Patti Perfect meets. The danger for many of us is in setting too many expectations for ourselves—expectations that are unrealistic and oftentimes trivial. Such expectations, coupled with failure to meet them, create undue stress for ourselves and our family.

The Gandhi Syndrome

What should we do when the stress and tensions of life begin to mount? What could a married couple do when one or the other experiences mental exhaustion? Suppose a wife, for example, needs professional help for her mental condition. Why is it that husbands are often hesitant to encourage, or in some cases, to allow her to obtain it? It may be because of what Dr. Mace calls the Gandhi Syndrome.

Like many other couples, Susan and I went to see the movie *Gandhi.* It was the story of Mahatma Gandhi, the Indian statesman. Millions remember him as a kind and gentle man, even a saint. Yet there is another aspect of Gandhi's life that is generally unknown. Dr. Mace relates that aspect in his book *Close Companions:*

The Gandhis were married at age 13, a marriage that was arranged by their parents. They had four children. Eventually in their marriage, Mrs. Gandhi became seriously ill. "The doctors diagnosed an infection that was spreading rapidly. Antibiotics were available, and preparations were completed for the necessary injection.

"At that point, however, Gandhi intervened. He believed that the body took responsibility for its own healing, and that no alien materials from outside must be allowed to invade it. All injections were taboo. He would not give his permission.

"The doctors argued, friends pleaded. But Gandhi could not yield. For him, a vital principle was at stake." That principle was that no outside help was necessary, no matter how great the need, when self-healing was possible. This philosophy might be called "The Gandhi Syndrome."

"So, while the doctor stood by with his syringe in readiness, waiting only for Gandhi's nod of approval, the infection spread and Gandhi's wife died." (Mace, *Close,* pp. 227-28.)

Gandhi's belief that the human body was always self-healing was sincere. But it was also erroneous. Help and possible recovery were available, but because of his belief, he was at least partially responsible for his wife's suffering and death.

Is there a similarity between the Gandhi Syndrome and attitudes held by some contemporary couples? I think so. We frequently read of individuals who refuse medical treatment for various reasons. But the same is also true with regard to mental health. Many people mistakenly believe that most mental problems are self-healing.

On this very matter I recently had an interesting conversation with one of my students at BYU. She was concerned not only about the physical health of her mother, but also about her mother's mental health. In fact, she believed that her mother's physical health was deteriorating because of mental depression. My young student was even fearful that her mother was near the point of harming herself and might even take her own life.

I asked my student if the family had sought professional help. She said her father was apprehensive about "allowing" his wife to seek help for depression. He thought it was a sign of weakness or "not living right," and that it might affect his standing as a leader in his civic and church groups.

The husband, you see, was one of those who believed that mental problems, in time, are self-healing. Even though competent professional help was nearby and available, he was willing to allow his wife to suffer. He ignorantly assumed that mental problems, unlike physical ailments, do not need professional treatment unless the people involved are "weak."

Perhaps the husband and Gandhi were correct in believing that some physical and mental impairments are, in time, self-healing. But many are not and are often fatal. When stress and tension become excessive, I think we are under obligation to "bear one another's burdens." (Gal. 6:2.) This may mean seeking necessary help.

145

How to Get Out of the Tension Trap

Are there ways we can learn on our own to reduce tension in life? I believe there are and would like to briefly discuss two. They are (1) develop a sense of humor and (2) cut back on some of our present activities.

Sense of Humor. If I were to list some characteristics of a healthy marriage, high among those on the list would be having a sense of humor. This does not mean becoming first-rate nitwits or engaging in the cutting sarcasm often depicted on television sitcoms. I simply mean we need to have the ability to laugh at the inconsistencies of life and not take ourselves too seriously.

I have recently read a fascinating book, *Laugh after Laugh: The Healing Power of Humor,* written by a physician, Dr. Raymond Moody, Jr., who is also the author of the widely read book *Life after Life.* In *Laugh after Laugh,* Dr. Moody gives an interesting account of how humor has implications for the medical profession.

In his chapter "Healing by Humor," he cites numerous case studies in which humor has either cured or helped to cure various types of physical and mental diseases and ailments. Most notable is the documented ability of professional clowns to help children and adults who are ill. Clowning, he notes, is a socially acceptable form of regression in which observers can revert back to the happier, more carefree days of childhood.

Dr. Moody gives a historical review of how humor and laughter have been viewed by various cultures. He quotes Proverbs 17:22: "A merry heart doeth good like a medicine: but a broken spirit drieth the bones." He also points out the destructive use of humor and laughter used by mankind to humiliate and degrade others. This kind of humor is debilitating. The physician notes that only when people can laugh together do communication bonds form. People are then often able to take a different and perhaps less serious perspective of life and its many problems. (Moody, pp. 17-27.)

Cutting Back on Activities. Many of us have been brought

146

up on the philosophy of never giving up on challenging tasks. We remember our high school and athletic events when we chanted, "When the going gets tough, the tough get going," and we often transfer this attitude to all areas of life.

We also remember the story of the two frogs that fell into the bucket of cream. One thought, "I'll never get out of here," and rolled over and drowned. The other frog kept on kicking and repeating, "I can do it. I can do it." With all his kicking and effort, he finally churned the cream to butter, and he hopped out.

It is an inspiring story . . . for frogs . . . who might fall into a bucket of cream. But have you ever stopped to realize that many people are consumed physically and mentally by constantly expending effort on difficult tasks they may never change? Or they ruin their health by working arduously on complex situations they may never overcome.

I am not an expert on trees, fruit, or pruning. But I understand one reason for pruning is so the fruit that is produced will be of better quality. Not only are the dead branches pruned, but often when there is too much growth, limbs producing fruit will also be pruned. Of this phenomenon Jesus noted, "Every branch in me that beareth not fruit he taketh away: and every branch that beareth fruit, he purgeth it, that it may bring forth more fruit." (John 15:2.)

Perhaps some of us need to prune the activities in our lives. Not only the "dead" or unproductive activities, but other endeavors may also have to be pruned so we can concentrate on just a few activities. Our time and energy can then be channeled to those few things we really want to achieve. As has been noted, a great challenge in life for Latter-day Saints is to not only choose between good and evil, but to also choose between good and good. There are so many good causes we can and often try to champion in life, but we may need to prune some of them out of our lives.

By pruning our lives, we can reduce tension and generate time and energy for a few activities, such as our discipleship of the Savior and our time for loved ones. This gives a new in-

147

sight to the related scripture "By their fruits ye shall know them." (Matt. 7:20.) Perhaps one of the great challenges in life is deciding what activities to prune back or out of our lives. In essence, when do we hang on and when do we let go?

If you are of the "never give up" persuasion, consider the following facts about the Danube River around Vienna. The Danube is beautiful and warm in the summer, and many Viennese go upstream and swim down the river through the pleasant countryside. But every year several people drown because they get caught in the river's whirlpools.

Drowning in the Danube River could be avoided if the swimmers only knew that all they need to do is hold their breath while the whirlpool pulls them down. In a few seconds the water will spin them out again. Instead, the unfortunate swimmers struggle against the current until they lose their strength and drown. The moral of this story reinforces the fact that we must learn in life when to hang on and when to let go. We must learn when to be like frogs that keep kicking in a bucket of cream and when to be like swimmers sucked into a whirlpool who must let go. We should not struggle against circumstances that could consume us.

Yet, a lack of knowledge of ourselves and our capabilities often drives us to do the opposite. We struggle when we should wait, and we wait when we should struggle. We waste energy trying to do what cannot be done and fight against facts of life that cannot be changed. If we do not become preoccupied with or resent the conditions in which we find ourselves, we can then focus on the areas of life in which change and improvement are possible.

In determining where we are going to expend our efforts and reduce tension, let us remember the prayer adopted by Alcoholics Anonymous:

> God grant me the serenity
> To accept the things I cannot change,
> The courage to change the things I can,
> And the wisdom to know the difference.

week. They are also supposed to pay genuine compliments, do good deeds, smile, and generally be helpful for the seven-day period.

Then there is what has become for many the most difficult part. Each day they are to touch the person in a nondemanding way. The students report that they can do everything else with ease except the touch. I explain that it does not have to be an embrace or even a hug. It might simply be just a gentle gesture of touching on the arm or shoulder. Even at that, some students have great difficulty in touching another human being.

One of my students, a muscular BYU football player, did everything in the self-esteem exercise quite well except for the touch part. He told me he was doing the exercise on his roommate, who was also on the football team. Finally, he said, the only way he could touch was to give a playful slap on the back as they left for school each day. I informed my student that he had completed the assignment. Even a friendly slap on the back was a form of touch.

Other students who have a difficult time with touch have developed something similar. They call it the "love punch." They will, in a jovial manner, give the other person a punch or jab as a gesture of saying "I care."

The tendency to be nontactual is both interesting and understandable with single LDS students. During the engagement and the early years of marriage, however, many of us touch our partners and feel comfortable doing so. But I am interested in the trend of marriages becoming nontactual after several years of matrimony. Many couples seldom touch each other more than what is needed for routine sexual relationships.

If I could encourage married couples to do just one thing to maintain or improve their relationships, I think I would suggest developing the skill of touch. Touch is one of the most significant forms of communication we have. Obviously, the absence of touch often communicates disinterest or lack of caring.

Many studies have observed that young infants in institutions can actually die from lack of touch. The phenomenon is known as *marasmus.* If young children literally need touch to stay alive, perhaps we never outgrow our need for touch as adults. The lack of touch between marriage partners is one of the contemporary traps in marriage, and marital marasmus can be deadly. One physician, Dr. Ed Wheat, has noted: "A tender touch tells us that we are cared for. It can calm our fears, soothe pain, bring us comfort, or give us the blessed satisfaction of emotional security. As adults, touching continues to be a primary means of communicating with those we love, whether we are conscious of it or not. Our need for a caring touch is normal and healthy, and we will never outgrow it." (Wheat, p. 183.)

Touch Is Also a Part of Sex

While many women, according to Ann Landers' survey, enjoy touch without sexual overtones, touch is obviously an important part of the sexual act as well. Perhaps a few thoughts on sexuality from an LDS perspective would be appropriate.

Several years ago when I was a young missionary for the LDS Church, I received a new companion right from the mission home in Salt Lake City. A few days later we were tracting and met a Protestant minister who invited us in. After exchanging points of view on various topics, he asked us, "And what is the Mormon attitude towards sex?"

I choked on my cup of hot chocolate, but my new companion seemed unmoved. "Well," said the minister after a few more sips of his tea, "could you please tell me the Mormon philosophy toward sexuality?" I was tongue-tied and believed my new companion knew next to nothing on the matter. There were a few more moments of silence, and finally my companion said, "Sir, we believe in it."

It has been more than twenty years since that time, and I have been asked the same question by numerous students, friends, professional people, LDS members, and nonmembers. Still, I haven't yet been able to find a better answer than the one given by the missionary: "We believe in it."

We believe in it inasmuch as we know of the sorrow and misery that come from the inappropriate use of sexuality outside the realm of marriage. We are acutely aware of what the prophets, past and present, have warned in these matters. As Alma declared to his son Corianton, "Wickedness never was happiness." (Alma 41:10.)

But we also believe in the good that can be derived from the appropriate use of sexuality in marriage. We are well aware of the love, intimacy, and joy that can come to a married couple when this particular dimension of the marital relationship is nurtured. An inquiry concerning the LDS philosophy toward sexuality seems more relevant today that it was when I served my mission several years ago. Much more is being said, and Latter-day Saints are being confronted with many issues on this topic.

In the United States today approximately 40 percent of marriages now terminate in divorce, and the inability of married couples to sexually relate to each other may be one of the major causes. Even in our own church, President Kimball has noted:

> If you study the divorces, as we have had to do in these past years, you will find there are one, two, three, four reasons. Generally sex is the first. They did not get along sexually. They may not say that in court. They may not even tell that to their attorneys, but that is the reason. . . . Husband and wife . . . are authorized, in fact they are commanded, to have proper sex when they are properly married for time and eternity. That does not mean that we need to go to great extremes. That does not mean that a woman is the servant of her husband. It does not mean that any man has a right to demand sex anytime that he might want it. He should be reasonable and understanding and it should be a general program between the two, so they understand and everybody is happy about it. (Kimball, Edward, p. 312.)

The sacred nature of the sexual act in marriage is noted in the book of Genesis. The first commandment to Adam and Eve was "Be fruitful, and multiply, and replenish the earth." (Gen. 1:28.) This commandment, and possibly an awareness of the process by which it would be accomplished, was given before sin entered the world. And this, along with all his other creations, was called "very good." (Gen. 1:31.)

A second commandment was also given that was related to the first. In Genesis 2:24 we read, "Therefore shall a man leave his father and his mother, and shall cleave unto his wife: and they shall be one flesh." Of the two commandments originally given, (1) to multiply and replenish the earth, and (2) to become one flesh, President Kimball, quoting the words of Billy Graham, has observed: "The Bible celebrates sex and its proper use, presenting it as God-created, God-ordained, God-blessed. It makes plain that God himself implanted the physical magnetism between the sexes for two reasons: for the propagation of the human race, and for the expression of that kind of love between man and wife that makes for true oneness. His command to the first man and woman to be 'one flesh' was as important as his command to 'be fruitful and multiply.'" (Graham, p. 118. As quoted by Kimball, Spencer, "Guidelines," pp. 7-8.)

The commandment to become "one flesh" is of particular interest to Latter-day Saint couples because it is mentioned at least six other times in LDS scriptures. (See Matt. 19:5; Mark 10:7-8; Eph. 5:31; D&C 49:16; Moses 3:24, and Abr. 5:18.) Husband and wife are encouraged to become intimate with one another. This intimacy or oneness might be described as a shared closeness that may be attained in a variety of ways, which includes, but is not limited to, sexual intimacy. For a broader perspective on the topic of intimacy, see *Human Intimacy: Illusion and Reality* by Victor L. Brown, Jr.

Some have believed that the only justification for sexuality in marriage is reproduction. While this may be the primary function, it is not the only important one. Another Church president, Joseph F. Smith, observed: "The lawful association of the sexes is ordained of God, not only as the sole means of race perpetuation, but for the development of the higher faculties and nobler traits of human nature, which the love-inspired companionship of man and woman alone can insure." (Smith, Joseph F., p. 739.) Similarly, President Kimball also noted, "We know of no directive from the Lord that proper sexual experience between husbands and wives need be limited totally to the procreation of children, but we find much evidence from Adam until now that no provision was ever made by the Lord for indiscriminate sex." (Kimball, Spencer, "The Lord's," p. 4.)

In a recent devotional at Brigham Young University, President Gordon B. Hinckley also addressed these matters, counseling husbands and wives to respect, appreciate, and love one another. (Hinckley, pp. 8-11.) "There can be nothing of inferiority or superiority," he said, "between the husband and wife in the plan of the Lord." He also emphasized that marriage is for having children as well as for companionship: "Much has been said on this campus about birth control. I like to think of . . . the meaning and sanctity of life, of the purpose of this estate in our eternal journey, . . . of the joy that is to be found only where there are children in the home, of the blessings that come of good posterity. When I think of these values and see them taught and observed, then I am willing to leave the question of numbers to the man and the woman and the Lord."

He also gave this rhyme of his:

> If I were you, what would I do?
> I'd live with my love with integrity true—
> And welcome our children, many or few.

Since our Heavenly Father created the human body and instigated the processes of reproduction and becoming one, it is obvious that both are sanctified by Deity and very sacred. But the fact that they are sacred does not necessarily mean they have to be secret. In reality, if LDS marriages are going to survive contemporary times, these matters should be dis-

cussed by couples who are married or those who are contemplating marriage. In this regard Elder Hugh B. Brown has
noted:

> Many marriages have been wrecked on the dangerous
> rocks of ignorant and debased sex behavior, both before
> and after marriage. Gross ignorance on the part of newly-
> weds on the subject of the proper place and functioning of
> sex results in much unhappiness and many broken homes.
>
> Thousands of young people come to the marriage altar
> almost illiterate insofar as this basic and fundamental func-
> tion is concerned. The sex instinct is not something which
> we need to fear or be ashamed of. It is God-given and has a
> high and holy purpose. Through the union of the sexes God
> provided for the perpetuity of the race. . . .
>
> We want our young people to know that sex is not an
> unmentionable human misfortune, and certainly it should
> not be regarded as a sordid but necessary part of marriage.
> There is no excuse for approaching this most intimate re-
> lationship in life without true knowledge of its meaning
> and its high purpose. This is an urge which more insistently
> than others calls for self-control and intelligence. (Brown,
> Hugh, pp. 73, 76.)

To young couples about to marry, the LDS leader counseled: "If they who contemplate this most glorifying and intimate of all human relationships [marriage] would seek to
qualify for its responsibilities; . . . if they would frankly discuss the delicate and sanctifying aspects of harmonious
sex life which are involved in marriage; . . . much sorrow,
heartbreak, and tragedy could be avoided." (Brown, Hugh,
pp. 21-22.)

Interestingly, Elder Brown suggests that sexuality to some
has become an "unmentionable human misfortune" or "a
sordid but necessary part of marriage." This attitude is obviously derived from a variety of sources that, unfortunately,
may include mistaken interpretations of a few biblical quotes.

In Genesis 3:16, for example, the Lord said unto the first
woman, Eve, "I will greatly multiply thy sorrow and thy
conception; in sorrow thou shalt bring forth children." The

present denotation of the word *sorrow* is distress, affliction, disappointment, grief, sadness, or regret. The word *sorrow,* however, had other meanings at the time of the King James Translation of the Bible. The Oxford English Dictionary lists care, anxiety, and pain as other common meanings. In fact, the Latter-day Saint edition of the King James Translation gives as a footnote the alternate translations of "increase thy discomfort and thy size" for "multiply thy sorrow and thy conception." In Genesis 3:17, where Adam was told he would obtain food "in sorrow," the footnote gives the meaning as "travail, pain."

The Lord indicated to Eve that with pain she would bear her children, not that conception or birth was to be a distress or time of grief. My wife and I have found, along with almost all other couples, that the time of birth is a time of joy and rejoicing. Yet, the mother must go through pain and anxiety to bear the child.

Another scripture that may be misunderstood in these matters is Ephesians 5:22, in which women are encouraged to "submit" to their husbands. Some have erroneously believed that women are to submit or yield themselves sexually to their husbands even if they do so unwillingly. Under these conditions, neither the thought nor the act does much to promote marital oneness.

It is also of interest to note that the words *sex* or *sexuality* do not appear in the scriptures. Yet the same process is described in holy writ with the words *know* or *knew*. It is recorded in Luke 1 that the angel Gabriel appeared to Mary and informed her that she was soon to have a child. Mary was obviously aware of the process of conception and logically asked the angel, "How shall this be, seeing I know not a man?" (Luke 1:34.) We are also informed that Joseph "knew her [Mary] not till she had brought forth her firstborn son: and he called his name Jesus." (Matt. 1:25.)

Elsewhere in the scriptures this same wording is used. It is recorded, "And Adam knew Eve his wife; and she conceived, and bare Cain. . . . And Cain knew his wife; and she

157

conceived, and bare Enoch. . . . And Adam knew his wife again; and she bare a son, and called his name Seth." (Gen. 4:1, 17, 25.) The biblical wording of "knowing" or "becoming acquainted with" is a beautiful way to describe the oneness that a husband and wife may attain in marriage through the sexual act.

Another example of a positive scriptural passage on sexuality in marriage was expressed by Paul in 1 Corinthians 7:2-5. Of this particular scripture, Dr. Homer Ellsworth has commented:

> Prophets have taught that physical intimacy is a strong force in strengthening the love bond in marriage, enhancing and reinforcing marital unity. Indeed, it is the rightful gift of God to the married. As the Apostle Paul says, "The wife hath not power of her own body, but the husband; and likewise also the husband hath not power of his own body, but the wife." Paul continues, "Depart ye not one from the other, except it be with consent for a time, that ye may give yourselves to fasting and prayer; and come together again, that Satan tempt you not for your incontinency." (1 Cor. 7:4-5, Joseph Smith Translation.) Abstinence in marriage, Paul says, can cause unnecessary temptations and tensions, which are certainly harmful side effects. (Ellsworth, p. 24.)

It has sometimes been suggested that highly religious people are so rigid or confused about sexual matters that their religious beliefs undermine their sexual relationships in marriage. This assumption now appears to be questionable.

Tim LaHaye and his wife, Beverly, surveyed 1,705 deeply committed Christian women with a 95-item questionnaire pertaining to sexuality in marriage. In their book, *The Act of Marriage: The Beauty of Sexual Love,* they reported that 81 percent of the Christian wives indicated they were "very happy" or "above average" in their marital sexual satisfaction. This was comparable to 71 percent of women who so indicated in another national study involving more than 100,000 women. This finding came as no surprise to the LaHayes. They wrote:

A Christian's relationship with God produces a greater capacity for expressing and receiving love than is possible for a non-Christian. The fruit of the Spirit (love, joy, peace, kindness, etc.—Gal. 5:22, 23) removes the specter of resentment and bitterness that devastates an exciting bedroom life. In addition, people who genuinely love each other will strive harder to please one another, become better informed, and treat each other more unselfishly. This will naturally enrich their love life.

We are quite satisfied that our survey has established that over the long years of matrimony, Christians do indeed experience a mutually enjoyable love relationship and that they engage in the act of marriage more frequently and with greater satisfaction than do non-Christians in our society. . . . It is a sad paradox that so many of those who have rejected or neglected God in their pursuit of sexual freedom and happiness often live miserable lives, whereas the Christian, whom they tend to despise or ridicule as being too "straight," enjoys the very things the non-Christian is seeking. It is our prayer that many who have not previously considered Jesus Christ will begin to realize the fact that He does make a *difference* in one's life. (LaHaye, Tim and Beverly, p. 196.)

I am also intrigued with a little book published more than forty years ago by Roy A. Welker titled *Preparing for Marriage*. It was one of the books used in the LDS Institutes of Religion for their course on courtship and marriage instigated some three years earlier in 1939. Under the topic of "Sane Sex Knowledge Important to Marital Happiness," Roy Welker observed:

Men and women engaged in human welfare work know full well the devastating effects of ignorance in sex matters. Fear, sorrow, a sense of guilt, often groundless, and sometimes disease have been the companions of ignorance. It is encouraging to know now, however, that schools, institutes, counsellors, and some families are recognizing, more and more, the need of sane sex knowledge as a preparation for future marital happiness. Reason and

159

common sense are coming to take the place of prudery and false modesty in dealing with the question. (Welker, pp. 90-91.)

Under the heading of "The Normal Functioning of Sex," Roy Welker notes at least three purposes of sexual expression in marriage:

> The question is often asked, "Is there a normal functioning of sex?" A negative answer would imply misunderstanding of the question, lack of appreciation of the purposes of sex, or a wilful desire toward sex perversion. *Wherever there are normal persons there may be normal sex functioning.* Evidently the first such functioning must be that of procreation. Likely no other means for perpetuating the race was ever considered. Did man institute it? No. Then God must have done so. This makes it a divine process. Should it not be so regarded?
>
> The next normal functioning is that of enhancement of personality. God has declared "man is not without the woman nor the woman without the man in the Lord." [See 1 Corinthians 11:11.] Men and women who have lived normally and happily together for years can testify to the personality contributions of each to the other in normal sex relationship. Those who have failed can testify to the personality deterioration they have suffered.
>
> In the previous section mention was made of spiritual values stimulated by the single standard. Another normal function of sex is that of spiritual unfoldment. This is a natural conclusion of personality enhancement and of thoughtful and purposeful procreation. A sane approach to the subject can find no other conclusion. *All the enduring values of life are heightened, taking on an added significance, when sex functions in its normal ways.* (Welker, pp. 93-94. Italics added.)

How to Get Out of the Touch Trap

You are caught in the touch trap if there is little or no spontaneous touch in your marriage other than for routine sexual relationships. To get out of the touch trap, try touching your spouse, as the opportunity arises, on a day-to-day basis.

It may simply be a touch as you pass by your partner; it may be a kiss, it may be holding hands, or it may be a hug or caress. It could also be part of sexual intimacy. For the importance of learning to be tender, reviewing "Trap 4: The Tenderness Trap" may help. Trying the "Three Ts" exercise discussed in "Trap 1: The Time Trap" may also help—along with time and talk, one of the three parts is touch.

TRAP 11

THE
TEMPTATION
TRAP

Temptation: Enticement or inducement, often through the promise of pleasure or gain, to do something regarded as unwise or wrong.

THE TEMPTATION TRAP: *Secret or questionable relationships with a member of the opposite sex that can lead to infidelity or adultery.*

ne of the most unusual trends in the area of marriage and family studies has to do with extramarital sex. In several surveys, 80 percent or more of those questioned indicated that sexual relationships with someone other than the spouse is "always" or "almost always" wrong, inappropriate, or sinful. Yet, even though the vast majority indicate it is wrong, a large number of husbands and wives become involved in affairs eventually leading to extramarital relationships—adultery, in other words.

How many married people become involved in extramarital sex? It is difficult to determine, but several studies have been done, with surprising results. In the early 1950s Kinsey reported that approximately 50 percent of husbands and 25 percent of wives had participated in extramarital relationships. During the 1960s 60 percent of husbands and 40 percent of wives were estimated to have strayed beyond the marital fold. Some researchers believed these estimates were high. Others thought them to be low. It is estimated by some today that in at least 50 percent of the contemporary marriages in the United States, one or both marriage partners will have sexual experiences after marriage with a person other than a spouse.

Do we know anything about those who do become involved in extramarital sex? Yes, we do. For men, it tends to be during their 20s. For women it is during the late 30s and early 40s. These years, respectively, tend to be the periods of intense sex drive and interest for many men and women. In addition, a woman is more likely to become sexually involved with a man other than her husband after the childbearing and nurturing years of children are over. The incidence of extramarital sex for males has also been found to be greater among the less educated during the early years of marriage. After many years of matrimony, however, the rate is greater among the more highly educated males.

Extramarital sex tends to be more common among the less religiously devout and among children of parents with very permissive moral values. People who have a number of sexual partners before marriage have a difficult time limiting themselves to one person after marriage. Most importantly, those couples with low marital and sexual satisfaction are more likely to look for other sexual partners.

How do extramarital relationships begin? Curiosity and desire for sexual variety, boredom, a need to reinforce self-image, a search for emotional intimacy, and a desire for retaliation against a marriage partner may all lead to adulterous situations.

What are the effects of extramarital relations on a marriage? We don't really need research to tell us, but one study of unfaithful wives indicated that 85 percent divorced their husbands within five years. Another study found that in over 90 percent of the marriages where extramarital sex occurred, the incident had caused emotional estrangement and lessened the sexual satisfaction within the marriage. (Stinnett, pp. 463-68.)

Flint and Steel

I was invited one time to speak to some BYU business management graduates and their spouses. I gave a few of my stirring remarks about the importance of balance between occupation and family life. (One fellow on the front row slept through the whole speech.)

At the end of my talk I asked if there were any questions or comments. One young man said he was a little perplexed about his forthcoming entry into the business world. He explained that his particular field of business management included many working women. As a married man, both he and his wife were concerned how a married man could or should relate to other women on the job. A married woman in the audience voiced similar concerns. How should a married woman conduct herself around her male co-workers?

We had a very interesting discussion of how the work world has changed. Though men and women have always worked together in limited numbers in the factories, farms, or offices, the number has greatly increased in our present soci-

165

ety. In earlier times, too, women usually worked in subordinate positions to men, but many of the men in the audience now acknowledged that they would be working with single and married women as coequals and that in some cases the women would be their superiors or bosses. In their business management training they had heard different opinions on how to cope with the new male/female relationships in the work world.

One philosophy was very cautious: Don't ever be caught working alone with a member of the opposite sex. That logic, extreme as it seems, does have some merit. I remember when I was a Boy Scout in Troop #561. Scoutmaster Mariel Hansen used to tell us that if we wanted to avoid fire, we should keep our flint in one pocket and our steel in the other. We followed his advice, and I can't remember any of us ever getting burned. There is a message there somewhere for men and women in today's work force.

The BYU graduates were also advised by others that times have changed. To succeed in today's business world, men and women have to learn to work together as peers and coequals. They wanted to know what I thought of that advice. I replied there was logic to that thought as well.

I shared an experience I had a few years ago when I was teaching at the University of Wisconsin-Stout. We had thirty faculty and staff members in the Family Life Department, divided nearly equally between men and women. We worked well together, and frequently groups of three, four, or five would walk over to the student union building for breaks or for lunch.

There were two young single women on the faculty. Both were in their late twenties, intelligent, attractive; and both also happened to be Latter-day Saints. The three of us often found ourselves going to lunch.

Then the thought occurred to me. Should I, as a married man in my middle thirties, be going out to lunch with single women even if it is job related? I thought about it and did what I believed was the only sensible thing to do. I talked it

166

over with my wife, Susan. She suggested we invite the two women over to our home so we all could become friends, and that would solve the problem for her. We did that, and I told the BYU group it solved the problem for me also.

To this day the two women (and now their husbands) are among our best friends. You see, I also remember something else Scoutmaster Hansen told us: Flint and steel can be carried in the same pocket if they don't get too close to each other.

Dousing the Spark of an Old Flame

If and when infidelity does occur in a marriage, it is often with another person known prior to the marriage, perhaps a former boyfriend or girlfriend. A young wife once wrote to me on this very topic.

> Dear Dr. Barlow:
>
> We have been married for about a year, and everything has been going fine except for one thing. I keep thinking about a young man to whom I was engaged before I met my husband. I find myself thinking about my former boyfriend from time to time and even dream about him on occasion. Is this normal, or is there something wrong with me? Does it mean anything about my present relationship with my husband?

Here is how I responded:

> You are quite normal, and your situation is fairly common since the vast majority of us usually become involved in one or two love relationships that do not lead to marriage. The impact of a former relationship on marriage, other than a divorce, is one of the most neglected areas in marriage and family studies. I have seen some young people become so devastated from breaking off an engagement that it takes them months to recover. Some never recover at all and choose to remain single the rest of their lives rather than risk the pain of separation again. After breaking up, some will quickly get into another relationship to show themselves, their former boyfriend or girlfriend, and often family members that they are quite capable of loving and being loved. Some of these off-the-rebound relationships

167

lead to marriage and frequently end up with disastrous consequences.

After marriage, some husbands and wives find themselves still attracted to other men and women. Whatever the cause, they feel that if they are attracted to members of the opposite sex other than their spouses, they are not now in love. Some have naively terminated their marriages only to find after another marriage that they still continue to be attracted to others. Rather than chase butterflies and seek happiness elsewhere, many of us should examine our present situations, learn to be content, and seek happiness in our present relationships.

Many married women, and I suppose married men too, retain mementoes from their former boyfriends and girlfriends. And if they do not retain the mementoes, they retain the memories. Some keep old love letters, pictures, rings, or gifts for sentimental reasons. When the present relationship becomes shaky, out come the items as a means of solace and a reminder that "someone out there once loved me, and perhaps still does."

While it may be normal to retain pleasant thoughts of a former relationship, we should be careful not to let them interfere with our marriages. The thoughts are usually harmless unless one chooses to constantly dwell on them. This phenomenon, known as psychic infidelity or mental wanderlust, can be highly disruptive to a marriage if one is frequently thinking about the former friend or wondering how a marriage to them may have been if things had worked out differently.

You need not try to totally forget your former boyfriend, nor need you feel guilty or ashamed because of him. The time you spent together was not a lost cause even though you did not marry. You both matured a little and contributed to each other's lives at that particular time.

But since you did not marry each other you should reexamine your present commitment to your husband and remember your wedding vows to forsake all others, mentally as well as physically. The combined efforts of both husband and wife are needed in contemporary marriage to meet the daily demands. Interests and energy invested in relationships with other members of the opposite sex can undermine your marital relationship.

If necessary, burn your old love letters from him if you still have them. Perhaps gifts and other mementoes should also be discarded if they are interfering with your marriage.

Be careful not to fan the spark of an old flame. While fire may provide warmth and comfort, it can also be consuming.

Love Must Be Tough

Dr. James Dobson from the University of Southern California has written an interesting book to husbands or wives whose marriage partner wants to leave the relationship. The title of the book is *Love Must Be Tough*.

According to Dr. Dobson, numerous husbands and wives face the possibility of losing a spouse through divorce, oftentimes for the reason of infidelity. Eventually about 40 percent of marriages do terminate in divorce. Many other married couples, however, consider separating without actually doing so.

What should one do when a marriage partner is giving undue attention to a member of the opposite sex? Many spouses become "clingers" or doormats and find themselves saying things like, "I'll do anything to keep you." Or they will allow, or at least tolerate, many clandestine relationships with the hopes that the wayward spouse will soon come to his or her senses and return to the marriage. This strategy, according to Dr. Dobson, seldom works. (See Dobson, chapter 5, pp. 44-50.)

No one can be forced to be in a relationship, particularly marriage. It should be started and maintained on some basis of spontaneity. People should be in marital relationships not because they have to, but because they want to. Begging someone to stay, or threatening certain behavior if they attempt to leave, only adds pressure to an already tense situation.

Many relationships operate on the principle of least interest; that is, the one least interested in the relationship usually controls the relationship. Telling spouses that you will do anything at any cost to keep them only puts them in control.

169

They then can do anything they wish, at any time, knowing they may return at their whim and at their discretion. Unfortunately, spouses in such marriages will take advantage of the situation.

So what does Dr. Dobson suggest to a person whose spouse is being unfaithful? Just as the title of the book states, he believes that love must be tough in that it has some parameters of what is and what is not acceptable. He suggests that a husband or wife living with a partner who wants out, or at least is not sure if he or she wants in, do some confronting. (See Dobson, chapter 7, pp. 58-69.)

First, declare to your wayward spouse your dissatisfaction with the present condition of the relationship. Be specific in pointing out what he or she is doing that you can no longer tolerate. This might include such things as dating or carrying on affairs with members of the opposite sex, excessive drinking into the early hours of the morning, staying out late at night, or not returning at all for several days. All these actions indicate a lack of caring on the part of the guilty party.

Second, declare your intent to stay in the marriage and indicate your willingness to work at the relationship under terms that specify a change in his or her behavior. By confronting your negligent spouse with the behavior you can no longer tolerate, you may think there is the danger of pushing him or her right out of what is left of the marriage. To the contrary, your willingness to work on the relationship under the new terms creates a situation with less tension and greater possibilities of staying together.

You also indicate your willingness to let go of the person if that is what he or she desires. Dr. Dobson believes in the old proverb "If you love something, set it free. If it comes back to you, it's yours. If it doesn't come back, it never was yours in the first place." (Dobson, p. 76.)

If you are facing the situation of a potential divorce because of infidelity, you may want to read *Love Must Be Tough*. It is available at most Christian bookstores.

The 3 R's of Infidelity

So much for what to do when your spouse is caught in the temptation trap. What about yourself? Like all other traps, this one is very subtle, and we often do not know when we are near it. But there are some indications when we are getting close.

In his book *Couples*, Dr. Carlfred Broderick, marriage counselor at the University of Southern California, noted, "Over the years, I have listened to the explanations of dozens of individuals who, despite such a commitment [for fidelity], found themselves involved in adulterous relationships. Again and again, their stories revolve around three issues which I have come to think of as the 3 R's of infidelity: *Resentment, Rationalization,* and *Rendezvous.*" (Broderick, *Couples,* p. 161.)

Resentment. Dr. Broderick reports that most married couples who become involved in infidelity are resentful in one way or another toward their spouses. Typically, they have not found a way to adequately deal with marital problems or resentments. The marriage counselor notes that the most important single prevention for infidelity "is a developed and well-oiled mechanism for dealing with strain in the marriage." (Broderick, *Couples,* p. 162.)

Another frequent source of resentment in marriage comes from the sexual relationship itself. Too often people enter marriage with high expectations, realistic or not, and when the expectations go unfulfilled over an extended period of time, resentment builds. Dr. Broderick suggests a married person then becomes a prime candidate for seeking a new relationship to find what he or she believes to be lacking in the present one.

Rationalization. If a married person committed to fidelity becomes involved outside of marriage, it necessitates some degree of rationalization. He or she first of all may simply deny or refuse to acknowledge the possibility of getting involved. A wife may flirt with another man and yet tell herself

171

and others it means nothing. Or, states Broderick, a husband may be high on drugs or alcohol, or may become inhibited and deny that anything will or could happen, even though it is already occurring. But the most interesting form of rationalization, according to Carlfred Broderick, is involved with virtue rather than vice. He notes, "I am convinced that more people get themselves into the pain of infidelity through empathy, concern and compassion than through any base motive. . . . With a little help from rationalization, the sympathy leads smoothly into tenderness, the tenderness to the need for privacy, the privacy to physical consolation and the consolation straight to bed." (Broderick, *Couples*, p. 163.)

Rendezvous. A rendezvous is a private meeting or an appointment to meet, and infidelity depends on a rendezvous if it is to occur. There are, however, some intermediate steps. Most extramarital relationships begin, interestingly enough, as friendships that "just happen." Two people meet at unplanned places such as work, parties, or even church. From these unstructured meetings they proceed to systematic associations that appear to be legitimate. There are more frequent meetings where they find excuses to be together for lunch "for business reasons." If the association involves two neighbors who find their friendship escalating, one may finally invite the other over when the spouse is gone. From these systematic associations, couples then plan and seek the private or secret rendezvous that is often associated with infidelity. And that is when it usually occurs.

Dr. Broderick concludes, "If you [as a married person] find yourself in a situation involving a delicious privacy with an attractive member of the opposite sex, you should begin to look for ways to restructure the situation. No doubt you will think of a dozen reasons why it is unreasonable to go out of your way to avoid perfectly legitimate and innocent companionships; but then, that may simply mean you need to review the three R's of infidelity one more time." (Broderick, *Couples*, p. 166.)

How to Get Out of the Temptation Trap

As a married person, you may be in the temptation trap if you repeatedly find yourself alone with a member of the opposite sex to whom you are romantically and sexually attracted. To get out of the trap, we have two role models in the Bible: David and Joseph. Both were confronted with potential temptation traps, but each one responded differently.

Pertaining to David, Elder Dean L. Larsen has noted:

> As a young man, David demonstrated a courage and a strength and power that likely has not been equaled in all of the great characters of the scriptures. He fought with wild beasts and overcame them, defeated the giant Goliath . . . , and then served many years as the leader of Israel. . . . The greatest enemy he had . . . was the man Saul. Yet on several occasions when David could have removed this threat by taking the life of Saul, who was in his hands, he withheld and controlled those impulses. That demonstrated tremendous power and control.
>
> Then later in his life, as a mature man with all the strength that kind of life had brought him, David was unwise. It was not because David was weak that he fell. He was unwise. I suspect that David had reached the point where he felt he was strong enough to indulge the entertainment of some enticing possibilities. On the day he stood on his rooftop and observed the wife of one of his officers, instead of taking himself by the nape of the neck, so to speak, and saying, "David, get out of here!" David remained. David thought about the possibilities, and those thoughts overcame David and eventually controlled him. (Larsen, "Thoughts," p. 121.)

Now contrast that with a similar situation involving Joseph and Potiphar's wife. We read the story in Genesis 39:7-12. Many are fairly familiar with all but one part of the account of Joseph's temptation. Most think it was just a one-time thing . . . that Potiphar's wife enticed him once and that he resisted. But in verse 10 we read, "And it came to pass, as she spake to Joseph *day by day*, that he hearkened not unto her, to lie by her, or to be with her." (Italics added.) Joseph's temptations were an ongoing occurrence. Because of his political and occupational appointment as overseer in Potiphar's house, Joseph could not just walk away at the first attempt of his master's wife. But when they were finally alone (a set-up she had probably arranged), Potiphar's wife made one last, desperate, inviting plea to Joseph. At that point he had no choice. He left his outer cloak, and as the scripture states, "fled, and got him out."

To those presently in the temptation trap, I recommend the "Joseph of Egypt" action: leave your coat and flee. Do what you must—if necessary, sever the relationship and refuse to see the person anymore. You may be strong and think you can continually resist . . . but then so did David.

It's your choice, your marriage, your consequences: Will you be like David? Or Joseph?

TRAP 12

THE

TELEVISION

TRAP

Television: The broadcasting of a still or moving image via radiowaves to receivers that project it on a picture tube for viewing at a distance from the point of origin.

THE TELEVISION TRAP: *The excessive viewing of meaningless or improper television programs during hours that could be put to better use.*

B efore I take television to task for its role in marital disruption, let me say some positive things about it. My minor in my bachelor's degree was in radio and television, and I have never lost my fascination with nor my appreciation for the positive influence the media can have on society. I was a weekly guest for more than a year on KSL Television's *Good Friends* in Salt Lake City and welcomed the opportunity to discuss different aspects of marriage on their program.

As a consumer of television, I have also appreciated many of the fine programs that have enriched my own life and also my own marriage and family. Obviously, I have enjoyed such religious programs as the weekly Mormon Tabernacle Choir broadcast and many of the other fine religious programs that are available. We have appreciated not only listening to LDS general conference on radio, but also the opportunity to watch it on TV. There have been many other wholesome programs on both educational and commercial channels that we have enjoyed watching as a family.

In latter-day scripture the Lord has revealed, "Yea, seek ye out of the best books words of wisdom." (D&C 88:118.) He also admonishes us to "study and learn, and become acquainted with all good books." (D&C 90:15.) In the dedicatory prayer offered at the Kirtland Temple, it was anticipated that "all those who shall worship in this house may be taught words of wisdom out of the best books." (D&C 109:14.) In other words, the Lord wants us to learn and be aware of what is going on in the world. (See also D&C 88:78-80.)

Since reading books was one of the main ways to convey information and ideas during the early days of the Church, the Lord simply expected his people to read and become aware "that ye may be prepared in all things." (D&C 88:80.) But he also admonished us to be discriminate in our reading, to read only from the "best books" or from "good books."

Had the revelations been given after the advent of television, perhaps the Lord would similarly have counseled to watch "the best" or "good" television programs and to also be selective in the programs we watch in order that we may become more aware and "prepared in all things."

Ways Television Can Disrupt a Marriage

In what ways can television harm marriage? I believe there are several. Every company that makes television sets ought to be required to attach the following label to each set: CAUTION: MISUSE OF THIS PRODUCT COULD BE HAZARDOUS TO YOUR MARRIAGE. Many believe that if we could get pornography and violence off television, there would be few other concerns to be considered. There are, however, also the following:

1. Television robs us of time that could and should be used in more worthwhile pursuits. Among those pursuits would be time spent with spouses and children, in reading and learning, or in some other useful activity. While documentation shows fairly conclusively that children today spend more time with television than they do with their school teachers, few have stopped to inquire about adults. It has recently been estimated that by the time we reach age seventy, we will have each spent about thirteen years of our lives watching television. This averages out to between four to five hours a day. And many of us are right on schedule.

2. Television is instrumental in attitude formation. More than just robbing us of our time, television robs us of our individuality in that we become the targets of multimillion-dollar mass motivation campaigns known as advertising. We not only dress, eat, and look alike, but we are now beginning to think alike. You may be saying, "Television really hasn't affected me or my family that much." OK, try this. How do you spell *relief*? (Hint: RO—.)

The capacity of television to reach an increasingly large audience was demonstrated on February 23, 1983, when more than 125 million Americans tuned in to the final episode of *M*A*S*H*. For two-and-a-half hours we were simultaneously entertained and bombarded with a few dozen well-timed and expensive commercials. Some believe that the

177

numerous commercials are now even more persuasive than the programs they sponsor. What messages are being sent to married couples? One television commercial I have wondered about features a husband and wife who are standing in a crowd. Someone walks up, looks at the man's shirt, and tells him he has "ring around the collar." Then his wife, mind you, apologizes for his dirty shirt. Why can't the husband wash his neck! The subtle message is that a wife is responsible for her husband's personal hygiene. How much babying and pampering do husbands need?

3. Television also conveys some interesting role models and attitudes on marriage and family life. A group of first-grade children in New York were recently asked, "From whom do you gain the greater satisfaction: your father or your television set?" The response? Over 50 percent said that if forced to choose between the television and ol' dad, they would choose the tube. That is scary.

Television can also be highly influential in determining marital expectations. Suppose someone is unhappily married and is a soap opera addict. Day after day he or she consumes hours of relationships portrayed on morning, midday, and now evening television. These relationships usually end in what I call one or more of the 4 Ds: divorce, desertion, disillusionment, or death. I seriously question whether soap opera addicts see many healthy marriage models during most of their television viewing.

4. Television helps make all of us, young and old alike, less sensitive to violence and pain. How many Japanese soldiers can we dispassionately watch get shot, bayoneted, or blown up with hand grenades on the sands of Iwo Jima during late-night television? If children view some 18,000 killings or murders on television by age 15, how many more will we watch as adults during our thirteen-year vigil of television viewing? Is television contributing to the ever-increasing violence present in America's homes?

5. Finally, television viewing disrupts daily schedules, family prayers, and/or family home evening. How many

home evenings have been held during the halftime of *Monday Night Football?* Because viewing habits differ, we also end up doing things at different times. Television affects the time we go to bed at night or get up in the morning and has likely affected the time for intimate moments of married life.

I would be willing to bet that if television viewing were cut in half, no one would suffer markedly. Married couples would then have the time needed to spend together talking, planning, or enjoying each other's company. American adults simply watch too much television. Surely there is a better way to spend thirteen years of our lives.

TEEVEE

In the house
Of Mr. and Mrs. Spouse
He and she
Would watch Teevee,
And never a word
Between them was spoken
Until the day
The set was broken.
Then, "How do you do?"
Said He to She,
"I don't believe we've met.
Spouse is my name.
What's yours?" he asked.
"Why, mine's the same!"
Said She to He,
"Do you suppose we could be . . . ?"

Anonymous

Television Can Sell Us a Life-style

On a similar note, Dr. Denis Waitley, popular author and lecturer on human behavior, has recently made these observations about the impact of television on our lives:

You have heard the old cliché, "You are what you eat." I would like to offer you a new one to share with colleagues and family members: "You are what you watch and think." A biblical expression in the Book of Proverbs advised us

179

long ago, "As he thinketh in his heart, so is he." [Proverbs 23:7.] Unfortunately, too many people exist on a mental diet of television, motion pictures created to shock us, and slick publications designed to stimulate us. I consider most of what we have available as "junk food" that leads to mental malnutrition and poor emotional and spiritual health.

Television is an extraordinary invention which should greatly improve our lives. Our world has been changed by television. You can turn off the TV set, but you can't turn off television's influence. We have been exposed to a wide variety of cultures and been given insights into life around the globe and in outer space. Television programs bring us athletics, encourage physical fitness, and provide many opportunities for learning about medicine, the arts, economics, local and world news, and religious events. The potential learning opportunities afforded by television programming are unparalleled in the experience of any pre-television generations.

The sad truth, however, is that because of the type of sponsorship necessary to support television in a free market system, very little broadcast time is devoted to stretching our minds, expanding our spirits, and enriching our understanding of ourselves and others. Much of the influence of television is negative. Many programs are dominated by crime, violence, and stereotyped deviant portrayals of people's lives. . . . Television constantly exposes children and adults to antisocial behavior performed by the incompetent, the uncouth, and the insane. At the other extreme are the superheroes with unnatural strength and superhuman abilities, who are beautiful and handsome. When average individuals compare themselves to their TV heroes, they usually see themselves as inadequate. . . .

We are growing up with television as our "window to the world" and the TV world has become the basis for many of our beliefs and values. . . . We can't really blame the television industry for the situation, because the quality of programming is only a reflection of the character of our families in the American social scene. But let's remember, if a sixty-second commercial, *by repeated viewing*, can sell us a product, then isn't it possible for a sixty-minute soap opera or "smut-com," *by repeated viewing*, to sell us a life-style? (Waitley, pp. 52-55.)

180

How to Get Out of the Television Trap

If you are watching more than four hours of television a day (17 percent of your time each day, and approximately thirteen years of your life), I think you may be snared in the television trap. Some individuals, families, and even whole communities have tried to quit viewing television totally— cold turkey—only to find it difficult, if not impossible, to do. Many of us are truly addicted to television viewing.

Do we need to cut out any and all television viewing? I think not, even though many well-meaning people have advised us to do so. As previously noted, there are too many good things on television that are edifying and uplifting to warrant throwing the TV out.

To get out of the television trap, I think we simply need to control our viewing. We should watch less television and follow the biblical counsel of moderation. (See Philip. 4:5.) If television viewing at first is difficult to control, we might put ourselves more often where there is no television until we develop more self-control.

We could also become more selective in what we watch by subscribing to a weekly or monthly television guide that gives us some advance indication as to the nature of the programs available for viewing. This would help us control not only the hours of viewing, but also the types of programs we and our family members watch. From a marital perspective, we should be particularly wary of the programs that portray unhealthy marital relationships in a positive light. Remember, many relationships portrayed in the movies or on television end in divorce, disillusionment, death, or desertion. And also keep in mind Dr. Waitley's caution: If television can sell you a product, it can also sell you a life-style!

A MARRIAGE
OF LASTING
VALUE

Value: Relative worth, utility, or importance; degree of excellence.

MARRIAGE OF LASTING VALUE: *A marital relationship that takes time to build, lasts through tribulation, and brings joy and satisfaction to the couple.*

L ike many other husbands, though I have good intentions to be a better husband, I don't always follow through. So one weekend I decided I had better practice what I preach. One of our favorite performers was giving a concert with the Utah Symphony Orchestra in Salt Lake City at Symphony Hall. I obtained tickets for Susan and me and made reservations in the Marriott Hotel across the street from Symphony Hall.

We had only minimal problems getting away. Tammy, our oldest daughter, agreed to watch the younger children. Brian and Jon said they would protest by riding their bikes up the canyon and spending a day shooting their BB guns. Jason and Kris agreed we could go if we would leave an ample supply of peanut butter and honey so they would not starve during our two-day absence. Our only major concern was our oldest son, Doug, who had recently received his driver's license. After a few white-knuckled rides, he had proven to me that he could, indeed, drive, and during our absence he offered to drive the rest of the children downtown in our other car for ice cream cones. Doubting his sudden altruism, we finally agreed, said prayers both vocal and silent, and left.

We arrived at the Marriott in time to change clothes and walk across the street to the beautiful Symphony Hall in Salt Lake City. We enjoyed immensely the performer and the numbers by the Utah Symphony Orchestra. Getting away as husband and wife is something we wait too long to do, and then we don't do it often enough. Perhaps other husbands are like myself: long on promise but short on delivery.

After the concert we returned to the hotel. Our room at the Marriott was on the 14th floor facing north. We had a spectacular view of downtown Salt Lake City late at night. Most impressive to me was the view of the beautiful LDS Temple on Temple Square, a building that represents to me the beauty and sanctity of marriage. As I looked at the temple late that night, I wondered why it was that the construction took forty years to complete. The temple that night also came to represent another important concept to me: It usually takes time to build things of lasting value.

Few people are aware of the destitute condition of the few thousand Mormon pioneers who started building the temple in 1853. Not many are aware that the pioneers had to start over on the construction project at least twice. The first time they had to start over was during the Utah War of 1857 when Johnson's Army threatened to enter the Salt Lake Valley. Brigham Young ordered the workmen to cover the foundation and encouraged the Saints in Salt Lake City to vacate the valley and move south. After the Utah War crisis was over, the soil was removed from the foundation, and construction of the temple was started again. Not long afterward, Brigham Young determined the foundation was insufficient and once more ordered the workmen to reset the foundation. He announced that the temple must stand for a thousand years, even through the Millennium. So they started over.

Building things of lasting value takes time and effort, whether we are talking of temples or marriages. If they are to endure, they should be built on a solid foundation, and their construction will require skill, time, effort, knowledge, and patience.

It may be that after a few years of marriage, we may face difficult times and be tempted to give up. But like the Mormon pioneers and the Salt Lake Temple, we may have to start over by working together again on the marriage. We must remember that things of lasting value usually take a long time to build, and things of eternal value may take even longer.

Diamonds in the Rough

I received a letter once from a distraught LDS wife. The letter from this particular wife asked a common question: Should I give up on my marriage?

To her and other married couples contemplating such a decision, I often ask another question: Would you be able to recognize a diamond in the rough?

There is an actual account of an African farmer who heard of the fortunes others were making mining diamonds. So he sold his farm and went in search of greener pastures. The farmer, however, was not very perceptive. He could not recognize diamonds in the rough. The man who purchased his farm did. The farmer had sold a farm covered with acres of diamonds that were still in the rough, uncut and unpolished.

There is also the true story of R. U. Darby, who was caught up with "gold fever" during the gold rush days. After weeks of mining he finally discovered a vein of gold in his Colorado mine and began to prosper. Then something happened. The vein of gold started to disappear. He had come to the end of the rainbow, and his pot of gold was vanishing before his eyes. Finally, he decided to quit and sold the mine to another miner for a small sum of money.

The new miner would not give up so easily. He called in an engineer to do some calculating. The engineer later advised the miner that the project had failed because the previous owner was not familiar with "fault lines" (an interesting analogy to marriage). The engineer's calculations indicated that the gold vein would continue just a few feet from where R. U. Darby had stopped digging. The new miner dug three more feet and found one of the largest deposits of gold ever discovered—worth millions of dollars.

Perhaps too many contemporary marriages are ended prematurely by divorce. I am aware of one recent marriage that lasted only twenty-seven days! In some instances divorce is not only an option but the only feasible choice remaining. Not all uncut stones turn out to be diamonds. But numerous married couples, particularly newlyweds, become easily discouraged and give up too soon on their marriage. With some more work and effort, their marriage may turn out to be something of immense value.

When you are tempted to look elsewhere for greener pastures, just remember someone else is probably looking at yours. And if another pasture looks greener, perhaps it is getting better care and attention. Grass is always greener . . . where it is watered.

What Matters Most in Life?

There seem to be a few times in life when we seriously reexamine our priorities. We determine what is and what is not essential. Those times often come when our own life or that of a loved one is in peril or jeopardy. I had my own moment of truth a few years ago.

During the early part of December 1970 I was asked to speak in Sacrament meeting during the Christmas season. At the time Susan and I, with our two small children, were living in Tallahassee, Florida, where I was working on a graduate degree at Florida State University. For my Christmas talk, I related a story contained in a book I had found at the university library. The book, *Precious Jeopardy, A Christmas Story,* was written by Lloyd C. Douglas.

The story is about a man named Phil Garland; his wife, Shirley; and their two children, Polly and Junior. Phil was disgruntled as he was driving home on Christmas Eve. He had just lost his job. As he arrived home, Shirley greeted him in her usual pleasant manner. But she, too, became discouraged as Phil told her he had lost his job. Their financial situation had been difficult even when Phil was working.

That evening Shirley tried to include Phil in some of the Christmas Eve activities with Polly and Junior. But Phil just grumbled at the price of the gifts. He reminded Shirley that in their tight financial condition they really couldn't afford any gifts. He said Christmas was overly commercialized anyway. Eventually Shirley helped Polly and Junior get ready for bed. Then tearfully she retired to their bedroom.

A few minutes later she heard Phil calling from the hallway. He yelled for her to get the pliers. "I've stepped on a needle!" he groaned.

Shirley brought the pliers, and Phil used them to tug on the needle protruding from his bare foot. Out came half of the needle! "That means," he muttered, "that the other half is still in my foot." He and Shirley discussed the possibility of his going to the hospital that night to have the piece removed. But Phil assured her it could wait until morning.

The next day, Christmas, Phil drove toward the hospital but then paused outside. Somewhere he had heard that if a tiny piece of metal gets lodged in the body and is not removed, it would eventually move to one of the vital organs and cause death. In his negative mood and after serious thought, Phil decided to leave the other half of the needle in his foot and experience the consequences. He drove home and told Shirley that everything had been taken care of.

From that moment Phil believed his life was in jeopardy, and he really didn't know if he would live from one day to the next. So he decided to make the most of life on a day-to-day basis. On that same Christmas Day there was a marked change in Phil as he treated Shirley with kindness and spent time playing with Polly and Junior. Phil had a pleasant Christmas Day with his family, but he didn't know if he would be alive the following day.

The following day did come, and Phil Garland found himself alive. For the second day in a row he was especially considerate to his wife and children because it might be the last day of his life. Each day thereafter, as Phil discovered that he was still alive, he was careful to treat Shirley, Polly, and Junior with love and kindness. He also took daily odd jobs in the community to financially support his family.

Precious Jepoardy ended, as it began, on Christmas Eve, only one year later. It was a sharp contrast to the previous Christmas Eve because Phil was so happy. He had lived long enough to celebrate another Christmas with Shirley and their children.

On Christmas Eve Phil played a few games and romped with the children. Before putting them to bed, they exchanged a few small gifts they had made during the year. During the last several months Phil had also made a lovely walnut sewing cabinet for Shirley. He took her to his work area and presented his gift to her. Shirley was again tearful, but this year it was due to Phil's thoughtfulness.

As the clock struck midnight, Shirley informed Phil that she also had a gift for him. She handed Phil a small box, which he opened. There, pierced through red velvet, was a tiny fragment of steel. It was the other half of the needle Phil *thought* was in his foot. Shirley said she had found it while vacuuming.

As I finished the talk, I emphasized the importance of people rather than presents at Christmastime. The Church members in Tallahassee seemed to have enjoyed the story. On other occasions in Florida I also related the story of *Precious Jeopardy*, pointing out the importance of commitment to and enjoyment of life with family members on a day-to-day basis.

After graduating from Florida State University during the summer of 1971, I accepted a teaching position at Southern Illinois University, and we moved to Carbondale. As the next Christmas season approached, I went to the university library, checked out *Precious Jeopardy*, and again reread the dramatic Christmas story. My appreciation of Lloyd Douglas and his story increased. But a few months later I had an unusual experience that would bring the message even more vividly to mind.

It was Saturday, March 4, 1972. I had gotten up about 5:00 A.M. to grade a few student papers. Later on that morning I was supposed to drive to St. Louis, Missouri, to a Church leadership meeting. Unknown to me, Susan had been sewing the night before for our little daughter, Tammy. Evidently Tammy had taken her new dress down the hall to hold it up before her in the mirror. She had unintentionally dropped a needle on the carpet floor in the process.

As I reached the end of the hall that early morning hour, I felt first a dull, then a sensational pain on the forepart of my left foot. The pain was so intense I dropped to the floor and grabbed my foot. Much to my alarm I found I had stepped on the needle! I called for help. Susan and the children rushed

189

from their bedrooms and gathered around me as I sat wincing with pain and holding my foot.

The whole event was painfully familiar. Susan got the pliers, and I pulled on the needle. It wouldn't come out. We agreed that I should go immediately to Doctor's Memorial Hospital in Carbondale a mile or so from our house. I found I could drive our station wagon even though I had a needle in my foot. Unlike Phil Garland in *Precious Jeopardy*, however, there was no question whether the needle should stay in or come out.

Still in my bathrobe and pajamas, I drove directly to the hospital emergency entrance. About 6:00 A.M. I limped into the emergency room and told the nurse on duty what had happened. She took me to an operating room and notified one of the physicians. The doctor arrived a few minutes later and did some preliminary examinations. Through X-ray negatives, he found the needle so deeply imbedded in my foot that he would have to call a surgeon to remove it.

The physician on duty instructed me to lie on the operating table until the surgeon arrived. "This is not a real emergency, Mr. Barlow," he said. "Maybe to you, it's not," I replied. He then left me waiting on the operating table for nearly forty-five minutes with no one else in the operating room.

During that time I got to do some serious thinking about the things that matter most when one believes his life is in peril. I immediately recalled my Christmas speech in Tallahassee just a year previous. What irony! I was living Phil Garland's experience! I thought that life is indeed precious, yet I had been so complacent. I had taken so many things for granted, including my children and my dear wife, Susan.

The surgeon finally arrived and began his examination of the needle in my foot. I asked, "Is it true that a tiny piece of metal in the body can eventually cause you to die if it's not removed?" The doctor smiled. "I think I've heard that before . . . but I'm not certain it's true. Anyway, you don't have to worry—yours will be out in just a few minutes." He then went to work to remove it.

Since the surgeon gave me a local anesthetic, I was conscious during the operation. I continued to think on the incident and couldn't help become a little philosophical about the bizarre experience, thinking that symbolically we all have a tiny piece of metal in our bodies called mortality. A biblical passage I had read many times again came to mind: "As in Adam all die . . ." (1 Cor. 15:22.) At that moment I fully realized for the first time that I, too, would eventually die.

After the surgery I returned home. My wife and children meant more to me than they had ever meant before. During that day and those that followed I began thinking more seriously about life: What were my priorities? To what causes and individuals was I committed? Where did I spend most of my time?

My foot eventually healed, but the vivid impression of that experience has never left me. Since that time several thoughts have helped me arrive at a philosophy, not so much about dying, but more importantly about living. Three thoughts have been particularly helpful.

The first is by Henry David Thoreau about the reason he went to the woods surrounding Walden Pond: "I wished to live deliberately, to front only the essential facts of life, and see if I could learn what it had to teach, and not, when I came to die, discover that I had not lived. I did not wish to live what was not life, living is so dear." (*Masters,* p. 405.)

The second, by Albert Schweitzer, has had great impact on my thinking: "The tragedy of man is not that man dies but what dies within man while he is living." (West, p. 216.)

The third is from the Book of Mormon. Amulek testifies that "this life is the time for men to prepare to meet God; yea, behold the day of this life is the day for men to perform their labors." (Alma 34:32.)

Our children are growing up, their grandparents are getting older, and we realize that we are getting older too. We hope we will be able to spend many more years together, for there are indeed many opportunities for rejoicing, renewal, reflecting, and recommitting.

I have located and purchased a copy of Lloyd Douglas's book *Precious Jeopardy* from a used bookstore in New York City. I read the book each Christmas season and think about my experiences, both those that are past and those that I hope lie ahead.

My needle is mounted on velvet and placed on our dresser as a constant reminder of the uncertainty of life and the importance of priorities and commitment in life. I have decided that foremost among my priorities is my marriage. Next is my family. And my most important commitment in life to a single, mortal person is to my wife.

Susan and children, I love you.

SEEKING
ADDITIONAL
HELP

I n *Traits of a Healthy Family* Delores Curran identifies one important trait of a happy family that many families overlook: "The healthy family admits to and seeks help with problems." (Curran, p. 257.) Many couples, including some Latter-day Saints, are hesitant to admit that they have problems and are even more hesitant to seek help in dealing with the problems.

For Latter-day Saints, LDS bishops are a vital resource in seeking assistance, and a vast number of families have been strengthened through their counsel. Usually the bishop can give the help the couple needs, but on occasion the couple should seek the help of a professional marriage counselor.

If outside professional help is sought, to whom should a couple go? Who is best qualified to serve as a marriage counselor? How much will it cost? At what point should consultation be sought? These and other questions are answered in a brochure entitled "What Is Marriage and Family Therapy." It is about the American Association for Marriage and Family Therapy (AAMFT), and much of the following information is based on that brochure.

A couple should first realize that not everyone who claims to be a marriage counselor has the training or qualifications. In states that do not license marriage and family counselors (Utah is among the eleven states that do license counselors), untrained, insufficiently trained, or totally untrained "lay counselors" are allowed to offer their services to the public. Unfortunately, in many communities outright charlatans and quacks prey on gullible and troubled couples.

Before starting consultation with a counselor, a married couple should seek one who is trained, and if possible, licensed; is willing to discuss fees in advance; will provide, upon request, his or her credentials as a marriage counselor; and is qualified and willing to counsel within the couple's perspective and value system. (Counseling by untrained personnel has been described as a process that often transfers biases from counselor to client.)

194

What Do Marriage and Family Counselors Do?

Marriage and family counselors today do more than merely deal with troubled marriages. Some specialize in family counseling, working with problems that confront not only husband and wife, but also parents and children. Other counselors specialize in premarital counseling to help young men and women prepare for the realities of contemporary married life as well as resolve differences that may already exist between the couple. An increasing number of counselors now offer divorce counseling, helping those whose marriages have ended to deal with their emotional wounds and to face the future with renewed confidence and hope.

Most people think that a marriage counselor will tell them what to do about their problems. A professional counselor, however, does not offer ready-made solutions or prescribe standby remedies. Seldom will he or she take sides or judge who is right or wrong. A counselor tries to help both partners deal with their own difficulties the best way they can and work out their own solutions.

When couples understand that a marriage counselor is not a wizard who has a magic formula for transforming imperfect marriages into perfect ones, they are likely to put more of their own effort into making their marriage better. To accomplish this, a marriage counselor may encourage the couple to look at their marriage more realistically and objectively, act as a neutral "sounding board" for complaints and dissatisfactions, help the couple identify the real rather than the reported problems, help a husband and wife realize how each contributes to the conflict and understand also that neither is solely to blame for the troubles, and act as a "mirror" to the marriage so that the couple learns to see it and themselves from a new perspective.

How Do I Know When I Need Marriage Counseling?

As a general rule, problems should be dealt with as early as possible. When couples wait too long to get help, conflicts

195

have escalated and attitudes have become more rigid and hostile, sometimes to the point where a major overhaul of the marriage is needed. Though timing varies from couple to couple, there are certain key times in a marriage when prompt counseling or therapy is vital. Some of these are (1) when a couple does not know why they are in conflict, or does not know how to change their ways of behaving toward each other, (2) when a marital problem is deeply rooted in a negative, personal pattern of one spouse, such as severe depression, chronic drinking, or acute anxieties, (3) when communication between a couple becomes almost entirely hostile, (4) when a couple cannot reach out to each other with love and understanding except with the support of a third party, and (5) when a marriage has deteriorated to the point where a spouse feels he or she must make a dramatic gesture, such as leaving home.

It is never too late to make constructive changes in a marriage as long as a couple want to make their relationship work.

Quite often, however, one of the partners doesn't want to see a marriage counselor. If one partner is reluctant, the counselor or the spouse after a visit to the counselor can often convince the partner to join in the process. When the counseling begins to produce positive changes in one person, the reluctant spouse often decides to find out what is happening by joining the sessions. And even if the reluctant spouse never becomes part of the counseling process, the support and guidance the other spouse receives is often helpful.

Counseling itself may take anywhere from a few weeks to a year or more even though there is a trend toward short-term treatment (six to eight weeks). Counselors in private practice usually set their fees on a per-session basis between $30-75 per session. Sessions may last anywhere from forty-five minutes to an hour and a half, and usually occur on a weekly basis. Counselors who work for social or tax-supported agencies may charge nominal fees, or none at all, based on family income.

Whether counseling will help resolve marital difficulties depends on several factors: how soon help is sought, whether both spouses are willing to cooperate for the necessary length of time, and how determined a couple is to make their marriage work. Experts estimate that about two-thirds of all couples are helped by marriage counseling, about twenty-five percent show little or no change, and the remaining eight percent report their marriage worsened. The measurement of "success" is difficult to ascertain and involves more than avoiding divorce. Couples have differing expectations of counseling and how effective it is. If a couple delays marital consultation too long, much of the counseling becomes little more than combat surgery.

How Can I Locate a Trained Marriage Counselor?

For over forty years the American Association for Marriage and Family Therapy has been the leading clinical professional organization in the field, with over 8,000 members. To obtain the names of those in your area affiliated with the association, write AAMFT, 1717 K Street, N.W. #407, Washington, D.C. 20006.

To find out whether an individual is licensed as a marriage or family counselor in the state of Utah, write to State of Utah, Business Regulation, Registration Division, 330 East 400 South, Salt Lake City, Utah 84111; or call 801-530-6633.

Counseling services for Latter-day Saints are available through LDS Social Services. LDS bishops and stake presidents have the names and locations of people providing these services. Further information may be obtained by writing to LDS Social Services, 50 East North Temple, Salt Lake City, Utah 84150 or by contacting a local LDS Social Services office.

WORKS CITED

Adler, Mortimer J. *How to Speak, How to Listen*. New York: Macmillan Publishing Company, 1983.

"Act on the Pinch." *ACME Marriage Enrichment* 12:10 (November 1984), p. 5.

Bach, George R., and Laura Torbet. *Time for Caring*. New York: Delacorte Press, 1982.

Barlow, Brent A. "Strengthening the Patriarchal Order in the Home." *Ensign*, February 1973, pp. 29-33.

————. *What Husbands Expect of Wives*. Salt Lake City: Deseret Book Company, 1983.

————. *What Wives Expect of Husbands*. Salt Lake City: Deseret Book Company, 1982.

Bartlett, John. *Familiar Quotations*. 14th edition. Boston and Toronto: Little, Brown and Company, 1968.

Black, Margaret B., and Midge W. Nielsen, "Patti Perfect." *Exponent II*, Spring 1979, p. 15.

Broderick, Carlfred B. *Couples: How to Confront Problems and Maintain Loving Relationships*. New York: Simon and Schuster, 1979.

————. *Marriage and the Family*. Englewood Cliffs, New Jersey: Prentice-Hall, 1979.

Brown, Hugh B. *You and Your Marriage*. Salt Lake City: Bookcraft, 1960.

Brown, Victor L., Jr. *Human Intimacy: Illusion & Reality*. Salt Lake City: Parliament Publishers, 1981.

Cuber, John F., and Peggy B. Harroff. *Sex and the Significant Americans*. Baltimore, Maryland: Penguin Books, 1966.

Curran, Delores. *Traits of a Healthy Family*. Minneapolis, Minnesota: Winston Press, 1983.

Dobson, James. *Love Must Be Tough*. Waco, Texas: Word Books Publisher, 1983.

Douglas, Lloyd C. *Precious Jeopardy: A Christmas Story*. Boston and New York: Houghton Mifflin Company, 1933.

WORKS CITED

Ellis, Albert, and Robert Harper. *A Guide to a Successful Marriage*. Holly-wood, California: Wilshire Book Company, 1972.

Ellsworth, Homer. "Is it our understanding that we are to propagate chil-dren . . . ?" in "I Have a Question." *Ensign*, August 1979, pp. 23-24.

Erdahl, Lowell and Carol. *Be Good to Each Other: An Open Letter on Marriage*. San Francisco: Harper & Row Publishers, 1982. As quoted in "Who De-cides What?" *Marriage Encounter* 12:6 (July/August 1984), pp. 10-11.

Gibran, Kahlil. *The Prophet*. New York: Alfred A. Knopf, 1955.

Graham, Billy. "What the Bible Says about Sex." *Reader's Digest*, May 1970, pp. 117-20.

Hinckley, Gordon B. "If I Were You, What Would I Do?" *Brigham Young University 1983-84 Fireside and Devotional Speeches*, pp. 8-11. Provo, Utah: University Publications, 1984.

Kelly, Burton C. "The Case against Anger." *Ensign*, February 1980, pp. 9-13.

Kiley, Dan. *The Peter Pan Syndrome*. New York: Dodd, Mead & Company, 1983.

Kimball, Edward L., editor. *The Teachings of Spencer W. Kimball*. Salt Lake City: Bookcraft, 1982.

Kimball, Spencer W. "The Lord's Plan for Men and Women." *Ensign*, Oc-tober 1975, pp. 2-5.

———. "Guidelines to Carry Forth the Work of God in Cleanliness." *En-sign*, May 1974, pp. 4-8.

LaHaye, Tim, and Bob Phillips. *Anger Is a Choice*. Grand Rapids, Michigan: Zondervan Publishing House, 1982.

LaHaye, Tim and Beverly. *The Act of Marriage: The Beauty of Sexual Love*. New York: Bantam Book, 1978.

Larsen, Dean L. "Marriage and the Patriarchal Order." *Ensign*, September 1982, pp. 6-13.

———. "Thoughts about Thoughts." *1976 Devotional Speeches of the Year*, pp. 121-22. Provo, Utah: Brigham Young University Press, 1977.

Lederer, William J., and Don J. Jackson. *The Mirages of Marriage*. New York: W. W. Norton & Company, 1968.

Mace, David R. *Close Companions: The Marriage Enrichment Handbook*. New York: Continuum, 1982.

———. *Love & Anger in Marriage*. Grand Rapids, Michigan: Zondervan Publishing House, 1982.

Masters of American Literature. Boston, Massachusetts: Houghton Mifflin Company, 1959.

Moody, Raymond A., Jr. *Laugh after Laugh: The Healing Power of Humor*. Jacksonville, Florida: Headwaters Press, 1978.

200

WORKS CITED

Murphy, Terry. ". . . As a Roaring Lion . . ." *Guideposts,* April 1983, pp. 16-19.

Novaco, R. W. *Anger Control: The Development and Evaluation of an Experimental Treatment.* Lexington, Mass.: D. C. Heath, 1975.

Olsen, David H., Joyce Portner, and Yoav Lavee. MACES III—Marital Adaptability and Cohesion Evaluation Scale. Third Version, 1985. Family Social Sciences, 290 McNeal Hall, University of Minnesota, St. Paul, MN 55108.

Olson, Terrance D. "The Compassionate Marriage Partner." *Ensign,* August 1982, pp. 14-17.

Pearson, Carol Lynn. "On Nest Building." *The Flight and the Nest.* Salt Lake City: Bookcraft, 1975.

Peck, M. Scott. *The Road Less Traveled.* New York: Simon and Schuster, 1978.

Peterson, Casey. "What Do I Need Today?" *Marriage Encounter* 13:8 (October 1984), pp. 4-5.

Peterson, Lawrence R., Jr. "What limitations are placed on Satan?" In "I Have a Question." *Ensign,* July 1984, pp. 30-31.

Pinnock, Hugh W. "Making a Marriage Work." *Ensign,* September 1981, pp. 33-37.

Roberts, B. H. "Elder Brigham H. Roberts." In *Eighty-third Semi-Annual Conference,* pp. 30-34. Salt Lake City: Deseret News, 1912.

Robertson, Alice. "Caring." *ACME Marriage Enrichment* 13:5 (May 1985), p. 5.

Smith, Ida. "The Lord As a Role Model for Men and Women." *Ensign,* August 1980, pp. 66-68.

Smith, Joseph F. "Unchastity the Dominant Evil of the Age." *Improvement Era* 20:8 (July 1917), pp. 738-43.

Spendlove, David C., James R. Gavaleck, and Val MacMurray. "Learned Helplessness and the Depressed Housewife." *Social Work* 26:6 (November 1981), pp. 474-79.

Stinnet, Nick, James Walters, and Evelyn Kaye. *Relationships in Marriage and the Family.* 2nd edition. New York: Macmillan Publishing Company, 1983.

Stuart, Richard B. *Helping Couples Change: A Social Learning Approach to Marital Therapy.* New York: The Guilford Press, 1980.

Swenson, C. H., Jr. "The Behavior of Love." In *Love Today: A New Exploration.* H. A. Otto, editor. New York: Association Press, 1972.

Van Leer, Twila. "Singleness Becoming More Common." *Church News,* November 6, 1983, p. 4.

Waitley, Denis. *Seeds of Greatness.* New York: Pocket Books, 1983.

WORKS CITED

Welker, Roy A. *Preparing for Marriage.* L.D.S. Department of Education. Independence, Missouri: Press of Zion's Printing and Publishing Company, 1942.

West, Emerson Roy, compiler. *Vital Quotations.* Salt Lake City: Bookcraft, 1968.

"What Is Marriage and Family Therapy." American Association for Marriage and Family Therapy, Washington, D.C. nd.

Wheat, Ed. *Love Life: For Every Married Couple.* Grand Rapids, Michigan: Zondervan Publishing House, 1980.

Ziglar, Zig. *See You at the Top.* Gretna, Louisiana: Pelican Publishing Company, 1975.

INDEX

exercise, 77-78; "Meeting of the Minds," 87-89; Communication on Spiritual Matters, 89-90; decision making, 98-100; Irritability Quotient, 123-26. *See also* Charts
Expectations, false, 40-42, 141-44, 178

Farmer-in-the-Dell syndrome, 123
Father Knows Best, 103
Fearfulness of marital disruption, 10-11
Feelings, communication about, 83-84, 89-90
Female: communication for, 82-83; supposed inferiority of, 95-97, 105-6; work relationship between male and, 165-67
Flattery is tactic of Satan, 18-20
Flint and steel, analogy of, 165-67
Forgiveness, 131
Freedom in marriage, 59-60
Frogs, analogy of, 147-48

Gandhi syndrome, 144-45
Garbage, anecdote about, 38-40
Garland, Phil, 187-90
Gaveleck, James R., 140-41
Gibran, Kahlil, 62
Girlfriend, former, 167-69
Gold mine, story of, 186
Gospel is key to resolving anger, 130-32
Graham, Billy, 154
Guide (model), 94

Haas, Adelaide, 82
Hansen, Mariel, 166-67
Harper, Robert, 122
Harroff, Peggy, 110
Head of family, 92-95
Healing, 144-46
Help, seeking, 144-45, 194-97
Hinckley, Gordon, B., 155
History, outlining family, 138-39

Horribilizing, 110-13
House painting, anecdote of, 136-37
Housework, 42-44
Humor, sense of, 146
Husband: and housework, 40-44; bonding between wife and, 58-60; selfish perception of, 63; profile of loving, 74, 150; communication for, 82-83; as head of house, 92-95, 105-6; can alleviate stress for wife, 140-41

I.Q. (Irritability Quotient), 123-26
Idealism in marriage, 108-9, 141-44
Identity, sense of, 59-60, 63
Impasse arbitrator (model), 93
Infidelity, 15-16, 164-65, 167-69, 171-72. *See also* Adultery
In-laws, problems with, 14, 117
Instinct and anger, 128-29
Intimacy through touch, 150, 154-55
Intrinsic marriages, 110
Ireland, divorce in, 80-82
Irritation, 113-14, 122-26

Jackson, Don D., 96-97
Jesus Christ, 71-72, 95
Job, decision about, 98
Joseph, example of, 173-74
Judgment, male, 95-97, 105-6
Jung, C. G., 4

Kelly, Burton C., 129-30
Kiley, Dan, 44-45
Kimball, Spencer W., 153-55
Kindness. *See* Tenderness trap
King (model), 92-93
Know, meaning of, 157-58

LDS Social Services, 197
Lagoon, example of outing to, 26-27
LaHaye, Beverly, 158-59
LaHaye, Tim, 131-32, 158-59